G000099487

TEACHING TODAY
pottery

TEACHING TODAY
pottery

Shirley Bates

Batsford Academic and Educational Ltd   London

To my family and friends for their patience and understanding whilst I have retreated to my den in order to write this book.

Acknowledgments

To Michael Whittlesea, who goaded me into writing this book instead of 'just talking about it' and for doing such splendid line drawings. To Jean Gilson for her expertise and advice regarding the photography. To Martin Brierley and pupils of Furze Platt Comprehensive School for the 'in school' photographs. To Chris Redknap, Warden of the Maidenhead Teachers' Centre, for his encouragement and help during my pottery teaching career. To Norman Luscombe who has so kindly written the preface to this book and been such a tower of strength to me as I have progressed. To all the schools and the teachers I visit who have inspired me to write this book and, of course, to Bert Hymus who has always provided the kilns and a 'yesterday' back-up service when urgently needed. Finally, to Thelma M Nye for her guidance and advice and for the interest she has shown in my ideas.

S B *Berkshire 1980*

© Shirley Bates 1981
First published 1981

All rights reserved. No part of this publication
may be reproduced, in any form or by any means,
without permission from the Publisher

Typeset by Tek-Art Ltd, London
and printed in Great Britain by R.J. Acford Ltd
Chichester, Sussex
for the publishers
Batsford Academic and Educational Ltd
An imprint of B T Batsford Ltd
4 Fitzhardinge Street
London W1H 0AH

ISBN 0 7134 39769

CONTENTS

PREFACE

One of the major differences that separates man from even the higher animals is his capacity to create. He is a tripartite being having head, hands and heart. Our educational system has laid considerable emphasis upon the development of the mind — helping pupils to become thinking people capable of asking questions and grappling with intellectual problems.

As far as the hands are concerned there is increasing recognition of the importance of practical competence. The heresy that craft skills are inferior to academic excellence is happily losing acceptability.

Sadly, the things of the spirit are almost invariably left to themselves. And yet, within man, there is a restless urge which longs for satisfaction and fulfilment. It cannot be denied that such a force exists and that it is potentially explosive. Realized it brings heaven on earth. Uncontrolled it can lead to vandalism, cruelty and selfishness.

Creative work in schools is so vital to give expression to this inner compulsion within man. Craft, design and technology is one area of the curriculum where the developmental needs of head, hands and heart are focused and can find simultaneous expression and fulfilment.

By working with clay and other natural materials pupils derive three main benefits. First, the sense of personal satisfaction, achievement and pleasure derived from mastery of materials and the exercise of skill and discipline. Second, having wrought with materials, the experience gained helps in the appreciation and understanding of the creations of others and must surely motivate against such evils as shoddy standards and vandalism. Finally, creative practical experiences must surely enhance the sense of wonder and intensify the appreciation of the work of the Great Creator — the source of beauty, truth and goodness.

It is with these views in mind that this book is welcomed to assist those who are involved in education through pottery craft.

N H Luscombe
Adviser for Design and Craft Technology
Royal County of Berkshire

INTRODUCTION

Is pottery an art or a craft? This question provides much room for discussion and I feel it would best be described as a mixture of the two. However, there is no doubt that it can be categorized as a part of design education. Design, of course, covers a wide field but much more emphasis and consideration is being given to design education today, particularly at secondary school level, than ever before.

When considering the production and design of craft pottery two aspects should be considered — the visual or aesthetic appeal and the practical and functional need. One cannot consider either one of these aspects to the total exclusion of the other as the result would almost certainly prove unsatisfactory. A good example of this would be an ordinary domestic pot which must not only look right but prove functional. On the other hand a ceramic sculpture must primarily be visually attractive but at the same time be made of the correct materials and by techniques that will succeed — in other words it must endure the processes of making, drying and firing without losing its original conceptual form. This is a matter of emphasis and priority. Costing is usually a major consideration and so volume and quantity of pots have to be thought about in relation to the equivalent kiln space available as well as the size of kiln shelves and props. The potter must also consider at the outset the number of processes involved in producing the finished pot. Of course, individual taste and preference must influence design but a satisfactory conclusion will only be achieved when all aspects have been considered and the problems solved.

The purpose of this book, together with others in the series, is to assist teachers in the field of craft, design and technology. It is necessary that teachers think and do before attempting to teach a subject and therefore this book is geared to assist those wishing to teach pottery.

It is my involvement over many years with teachers and children and their particular needs in the field of pottery that has caused me to produce this handbook. There are, indeed, many very good pottery books on the market but none, I find, that really simplify the problems the teacher faces in the classroom situation — this is what this handbook is about. It is my answer to the many cries I receive for help — and I hope it will eliminate the underlying fear that some teachers have when contemplating the teaching of pottery and the firing of a kiln.

This handbook is not intended to demonstrate the large variety of techniques for the actual making of pottery but will, I hope, explain in simple terms the techniques involved surrounding the making of a pot.

I would like to emphasize that in this handbook I do not attempt to explain the only method of doing something — simply the techniques that I find most suitable and convenient, taking into account the limited availability in most schools of finance, materials, equipment, space and sizes of groups. However, in spite of all the obstacles met in the teaching of pottery, it must be one of the most rewarding subjects in the whole curriculum — the children love it, the teachers love it and the mums love it! We must also remember the incredible therapeutic value of working with clay — for people of all ages. I have encountered children who are severely withdrawn for various reasons but who improve considerably when encouraged to work with clay. It is all a matter of success — a little can go a long way — and this, then, is the purpose of this book — to help the teacher help the pupil to make a success of his pottery. With a foot on the first rung of the success ladder, many doors may open, it is all a matter of confidence.

I am quite sure that to succeed in the teaching of a practical subject the teacher must have the necessary practical background knowledge, for without this the end products will suffer and the design advantage of the subject will soon cease to exist.

It is intended that the 'hobby potter' too, will find this handbook useful as its aim is to provide, as simply as possible, the basic working guidelines for those wishing to teach and do pottery.

Approximate conversions
1 kg = 2.2 lbs
1 litre = 2.1 pts
1 cm (10 mm) = 0.4 ins
1 m = 3.3 feet

A pot for Mum!

1 The classroom

'The head has asked me to take responsibility for the teaching of pottery in this school'. I have heard this many times and consequently received pleas for help. What do I teach? What do I need to order? How many children can I teach pottery to at one time? Is my kiln alright and how do I fire it? How do I mix a glaze? How do I start the children off? How do I get success?

Materials and tools

To start with we must consider the materials and equipment needed to teach pottery. Of course, these needs must vary according to the age groups being taught and time allowed on the curriculum. Fortunately many useful items can usually be collected from looking around the school, at home and especially from local jumble sales. However, some items must be purchased from pottery suppliers and such essentials are:

Kiln — with safety lock and guard, shelves and props.
Clay — 200 kg general purpose grey clay
    50 kg terra cotta clay (red)
    (this can usually be purchased through county stores)
25 kg plaster of paris
10 kg transparent glaze (earthenware)
5 kg opaque white glaze (earthenware)
5 kg china clay
5 kg ball clay
½ kg Bentonite
½ kg bat wash
2½ kg silica sand
2½ kg manganese dioxide
2½ kg red iron oxide
½ kg iron oxide — yellow ochre
½ kg copper carbonate
½ kg cornflower blue or turquoise blue stain
1 box disposable masks
1 lawn brush
1 lawn (sieve) 80 mesh
1 lawn (sieve) 120 mesh
50 cones 04 ⎱
50 cones 07 ⎰ (if there is no pyrometer with the kiln)

Useful extras where funds permit:
1 set of 6 boxwood tools
1 set of 5 wire ended tools
2 fine needles
2 rubber kidneys
2 metal kidneys

Pottery students at work in the classroom

2 sets of turning tools if you possess a wheel
1 harp
1 spare wire for harp
1 square tile cutter
1 hexagonal tile cutter
1 round tile cutter
2 slip trailers
1 lightweight aluminium whirler
1 set of balance scales
2 108 mm funnels
2 large polythene bins with clip on lids.
Plastic dustbins (two for each type of clay)

As already mentioned many useful items can be collected for little or no cost – parents are often very willing to assist in this way. Such items to ask for include:

buckets, washing-up bowls, jugs, funnels, 2.5 litre and 5 litre containers (plastic), large storage jars with screw top lids, coarse cup-type sieves, broomsticks (for cutting up to make rolling pins), cutlery (old knives forks and spoons), dustbins (metal or plastic), plastic hair treatment bottles for use as slip trailers, wooden slats 32 mm wide x 6 mm thick for use as rolling guides, card centres of toilet rolls and carpet rolls, polythene bread bags and ties, pieces of sponge, small pieces of board, or beer mats for placing pots on, newspaper, lollipop sticks, sacking or pieces of linen for rolling clay on, fishing line and buttons for making wire cutters.

Pupil organization

In addition to the above I have found it a great advantage, for smoothness of classroom organization, for each pupil to have his own kit. This can be collected by each individual at virtually no cost and if kept in a named box can be stored in a corner of the classroom, a cupboard or a locker and be available when required. This eliminates the problem of finding there are insufficient tools in the classroom stock for all to use at one time. Particularly at primary level, a child who has his own tool kit to hand will be much keener to integrate claywork into a variety of subjects instead of always waiting for the 'clay lesson' to implement his ideas – for example he may well make a castle or a totem pole in a history lesson, a leaf or a bird in a nature lesson or even weigh out clay in a maths lesson! At secondary level it is even more important that pupils possess their own kit — particularly those specializing. This relates to a craftsman possessing and caring for his own tools and, above all, knowing them. Another advantage, of course, is that with present day financial cut backs, available money can be spent on materials such as glazes and oxides which must be financed from the central fund. The addition of a larger variety of these materials will enhance the beauty and variety of the pottery that can be made. This system eliminates the irritation caused by having to wait around for certain tools and it also prevents pupils stretching over another person's work to 'borrow' a tool — this is when work is damaged and pots of water and oxides are easily spilt. A pupil's concentration is greatly improved when his tools are to hand and consequently his standard of work will improve.

I list below the items I recommend pupils to collect. With younger children it is a good idea to allow them a period of time for collecting their kit and then to award effort marks or 'stars' — it's amazing how rapidly they will produce their kit and the enjoyment they experience in so doing.

Tool kit

Overall (an old shirt worn back to front is ideal)
Shoe box, plastic container or biscuit tin — named! containing:
6 — 12 lollipop sticks
old knife, fork and spoon
kitchen scourer or a piece of fine sandpaper
small piece of sponge
thin paint brush
356 mm fishing line or thin wire for cutting clay
a few decorative buttons
cloth for rolling clay on (hessian or sheeting 356 x 457 mm)
card centre of toilet roll
needle in a cork — for fine cutting out
knitting needle
2 polythene bags with ties (eg bread bags and ties)
rolling pin (optional) or 305 mm piece of broom handle
All the above items should comfortably fit into an average sized shoe box or container and if clearly named will be easily recognizable when required. The teacher will, of course, find it helpful to keep a master kit containing several of each of the above items. As for the tools that the teacher may have ordered from suppliers I would recommend that these are kept on a shadow board as they are expensive and if replaced in this way after use their life will be considerably longer. I would also strongly recommend that pottery tools should not be used for other craft subjects or they will soon be damaged and become useless.

Useful tips

As in most practical subjects there are many useful tips that one collects over the years and I give below some of those that I have found to be most helpful in the classroom situation:

(a) Make sure that each pupil inscribes or paints with oxide onto the base of his pot his initials and class number. This should be done before biscuit firing and will save many upsets and headaches for the teacher when the cry 'he's got my pot' issues forth. To children pots often change out of all recog-

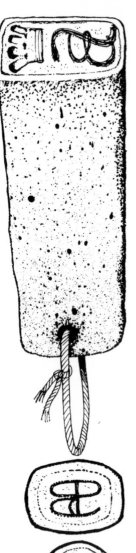

nition once they have been glazed and fired! A more sophisticated method that I encourage older students to adopt is to make a signet block from clay and inscribe their initials in reverse on it. (A credit card with its raised lettering can produce very neat lettering when pressed into clay.) The block must be fired to biscuit temperature and if kept in the tool kit can be used to stamp all pottery — in the same way as signet rings were used on wax years ago. If a string needs to be attached to the block, make a hole through one end before firing and it is a good idea to inscribe one's full name on the side of the block for easy recognition.

(b) Thread medium sized buttons onto the ends of the pieces of wire or fishing line to be used for cutting clay. These will add weight to the wires enabling them to be hung up and not so easily lost. Brightly coloured buttons also help to keep the wire visible.

(c) Encourage pupils to keep the spare clay they are working with protected under polythene. If it is left uncovered on the bench it will tend to dry and often becomes impossible to work with. It is also advisable to see that 'crumbs' of clay are not left around — mop them up with a larger ball and keep it under cover. In heated classrooms the problems of small pieces of clay drying rapidly can cause unnecessary frustration.

(d) If clay is rather hard to use, slice it up, sprinkle with a little water, wrap up in polythene and leave for a while — as long as it was only a little too hard it will soon soften again.

(e) When rolling out clay in a warm drying atmosphere it often helps to roll it onto a cloth that has been slightly dampened — the clay will then soften as it is rolled.

(f) If clay is too soft to work, knead it on a plaster bat or a soft wooden table-top or board — the excess water will then be absorbed by the plaster or wood.

(g) Always encourage pupils, *as a habit*, to wedge and knead their clay before starting work — and to prick out any air bubbles.

(h) Do not use more water than is absolutely necessary for handbuilding techniques — it only turns clay into mud and makes it collapse. A little natural slip for joining seams is all that should be required — keep jars of this slip or water small, then they are less likely to spill!

(i) Beware of damage that can be caused by sanding clay when in its brittle dry state — it is often safer to smooth with a damp sponge, preferably at an earlier stage.

(j) Whenever possible prepare clay before the lesson commences, particularly where large groups are concerned. It is wise to make it up into balls and store in a sealed bin. Boys often really enjoy this chore.

(k) Never hurry work — it is far better to produce one good piece of work in a term than ten shoddy pieces.

A potter's stamp

(l) With younger children, in particular, I recommend that after the first piece of each child's work has been fired, only the best work that each child produces should be fired on future occasions. In this way their standard of work will improve and you will not be overloaded with a large backlog of pottery needing to be fired — the firing and glazing of a pot then becomes a form of praise or merit for good work. Remember that clay which has not been fired (however dry) can always be reconstituted and so be used again.

Partially finished monster

The classroom or studio

If clay is to be worked in an area designed for the purpose then the problems of suitable benches and the proximity of sinks and water do not occur. However, in primary schools these facilities are not always available so the following recommendations may well be of assistance:

(a) Try to govern the size of a group doing clay by their 'elbow space'. Provided children have their tool kits at hand quite large groups can do clay work quite satisfactorily.

(b) Whenever possible allow children to work outside, but out of the direct sun or their clay will dry rather rapidly.

(c) Ensure children using clay are covered adequately by overalls.

(d) Desks and tables need to be covered — newspaper and pieces of hessian or sheeting for rolling on — boards or trays can also be useful. I have found, too, that kitchen-cloths are very suitable for rolling out clay on and are also useful for mopping up later — they wash out and dry quickly.

(e) Insist that each pupil (whatever his age) cleans up his own area before the end of the lesson. It is advisable to do an overall check before the room is vacated and to check bottoms of shoes as clay can be carried all over the place by feet!

(f) If there is no sink in the classroom then have a bucket or two of water in the classroom for hand washing otherwise door handles tend to get covered in clay! If there are taps and a sink check that these are not choked with clay at the end of the lesson.

(g) Lastly, I would recommend that children are reminded to go to the toilet before the clay lesson starts.

Stimuli

It is extremely advantageous to provide various forms of stimuli in and around a room in which claywork is to take place. I give below examples that I have found pupils to be particularly responsive to:

(a) *Shells:* a collection should be made and regularly added to as they stimulate not only ideas of shape, form and colour but also texture. They can be sketched, built up into compound forms to create new shell shapes and

13

Owls made after a bird study

used to texture the clay by pressing them into it or scratching them across its surface.

(b) *Bark* from various trees and shrubs makes a very interesting study. The colours vary from silvers and greys, greens and yellows to browns and blacks. All these colours can be simulated with oxides and stains. The textures of various barks are even more fascinating and if clay is rolled out over a large piece of bark before the pot is constructed the effect is quite amazing — the clay really does look like the bark.

(c) *Stones and rocks:* a collection can usually be kept outside the classroom but is extremely useful to have to hand for copying purposes and for the study of the textures and colours which vary enormously, particularly in section.

(d) *Animals:* in many primary school classrooms animals are kept in cages as class pets and these are ideal models for claywork as children are well acquainted with their movements and expressions and translate these very well into claywork. Classroom pets usually consist of hamsters, gerbils, mice, guinea pigs, rabbits, etc, but on occasion I have seen larger animals imported for children to study such as a cockerel which was placed in a large pen and a sheepdog who obediently sat still for a whole lesson. In one school I visited there was a beautifully coloured parrot for the children to look at. These children had also recently been to a local bird sanctuary and their clay models were very impressive. The fact that they had been able to study live animals instead of just pictures of them had helped them to put life into their claywork in an uncanny way. These children really managed to capture the expression and movement of the birds they had studied and this, of course, will most certainly apply to the work done by children who study any other form of life — even themselves! Earlier in this chapter I mentioned the advantage of integrating claywork with other subjects and live models certainly provide a very good stepping stone for the imaginative teacher.

Suppliers

At the end of this book I have listed the names and addresses of recommended educational suppliers. Although I tend to favour materials supplied by Podmores, this is really a matter of personal preference and each teacher and potter must choose for himself.

14

2 Safety in the classroom

The Health and Safety at Work Act (1974) demands that all pottery areas in schools shall conform to required standards. The practical interpretation of this act causes confusion in the minds of many teachers and in this chapter I shall hope to explain it and suggest a commonsense approach.

Pottery kilns

The regulations regarding kilns are the most stringent of all as the kiln is, without doubt, potentially the most dangerous piece of equipment unless these basic rules are observed:

1 No kiln may be sited, or resited, and installed without the local fire officer's prior approval.

2 It should be noted that no teacher should use a pottery kiln without first having been instructed in the procedures to be followed by the supplier, an adviser or an experienced pottery teacher.

3 Arrangements should be made for a local electrical contractor, who has experience of kilns and their operation, to check their electrical and mechanical safety. This service should be arranged on an annual basis.

4 Kilns should be provided with the following:
    (a) Automatic cut-out devices fitted to all doors.
    (b) Interlocking key switches which prevent the kilns being opened when the mains supply is on. The key which controls the lock should be kept in the charge of the pottery teacher and be placed out of reach of children. It is recommended that it be kept near the kiln but high up for if it is lost (and each lock is supplied with only one) it is a lengthy process to obtain a dupli-

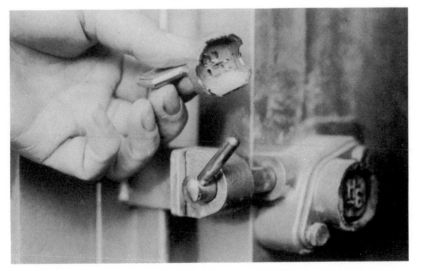

Castell interlock and key

Pyrometer

cate – it would incur a special order being placed with the kiln manufacturer and, of course, the kiln would be out of use until the key is replaced.

(c) Individual red warning lamps should be fitted, with two bulbs, mounted at high level above the kilns and linked to the mains isolating switches.

(d) Suitable guards to prevent the unauthorized removal of bungs or accidental contact with the kiln casing – these should be provided where kilns are located in teaching areas. If the kiln is sited in a separate cupboard or room without a guard surrounding it, then the door to this room or cupboard must be fitted with a lock and key *and* a second red warning lamp must be sited on the outside of this room or cupboard to indicate when the kiln is being fired.

5 Adequate ventilation is necessary, such as an extractor fan, an opening window or door grid in the kiln area.

6 Overfiring of kilns: there are various methods of preventing such an occurrence, ie

(a) The addition of a heat fuse, a mini controller or a time clock.

(b) A log should be kept of firing times and a routine firing timetable should be adopted.

(c) The caretaker should be asked to check that the temperature of the kiln is 'low' (by cone, simmerstat or pyrometer) if a kiln light is seen to be switched on at the end of the day. To assist, always place a sign on top of the kiln indicating that the kiln is on 'low' and describing the type of firing, eg kiln on low – 960°C. In this way if the person in charge of the kiln is absent the next day the kiln may still be fired to its completion without spoiling the contents.

7 Children must not be permitted to touch a hot kiln or to open a kiln, even if cold, unless under a teacher's supervision.

8 A carbon dioxide fire extinguisher should be fixed to a wall near to the kiln so that it is easily accessible.

Pug mills

These are not considered necessary equipment for primary schools but in secondary schools where they are often used they must be fitted with the following:

(a) A wall mounted isolator switch.

(b) A key operated switch – the key to be removed to prevent unauthorized use when idle.

(c) A waterproof NV/OL push button starter switch.

(d) The machine must have adequate guards to cover all pulley drives and gears, and finger grills or guards must be positioned at the bottom of the loading holes. Should a pugmill be found to be without a finger guard it must be taken out of use until a suitable guard has been obtained from the manufacturer of the machine and fitted.

(e) It is recommended that only teachers or senior students, under direct supervision, should operate a pugmill.

Wheels

These should be serviced regularly and power wheels should be carefully sited close to suitable socket outlets in order to reduce the necessity for long

16

leads. Waterproof push button starters (NV/OL type) should be fitted. A useful tip for protecting the wall plug and socket from being touched by wet fingers or being clogged by clay is to place the plug in a polythene bag and then plug it into the socket – a simple idea but it works!

Hair: if students using wheels have long hair do ensure that they tie it back securely to prevent it getting caught up in the revolving wheelhead.

Spray booths

Spray booths must be correctly installed and vented to the atmosphere. Filters must be replaced or washed out regularly. If compressed air equipment is used it must be serviced regularly and carry a manufacturer's certificate of worthiness indicating safe working pressure. It must be inspected annually by an approved authority and only used by those with experience or under strict supervision.

NB It is important that all equipment be used only by those with experience in the correct operating procedures or under the strict supervision of such people.

Pottery materials

Lead free materials *only* should be used unless the teachers concerned have attended approved courses in pottery craft or are ceramics specialists.

Oxides and stains: most oxides and stains, if purchased from a reputable educational supplier and handled sensibly, are safe. However, mention should be made regarding the use of copper based oxides and stains ie the green ones. If these colours are used with low-solubility lead glazes the lead release is increased making the glaze unsuitable for use with foodstuffs and beverages which are slightly acid, such as lemon juice. In simple terms, keep greens for ornamental pottery and on vessels that are unlikely to come into contact with foods or acids – play safe!

Glazes: teachers are advised to buy ready-mixed glazes in the lead-free and low-lead-solubility ranges and *not* to attempt mixing their own glazes from raw materials unless trained to do so. An exception to this rule is the ash glaze but, even here, care is needed for ash mixed with water is caustic and can cause minor skin irritation – use rubber gloves when mixing them.

Masks: when mixing glazes or slips it is advisable to wear a simple mask to prevent inhalation of dust. Masks similar to the type nurses use can be purchased quite cheaply in boxes (similar to paper tissues) from large chemists. When sanding a dry pot it is best to do this over a bowl of water as this will absorb much of the flying dust.

Glass: broken pieces of coloured glass make a very attractive decoration to the bottom of a bowl or pot when fused with the glaze. However, I have heard of shocking accidents where children have been allowed to break the glass into small pieces without adequate supervision. Ideally the teacher should do this job – preferably outside with nobody else around. The bottle or glass to be broken should be wrapped in several sheets of newspaper and a cloth, before hitting it with a hammer. It is advisable to wear glasses for extra protection as the eyes are most vulnerable – a tiny splinter can cause severe eye damage. When the pieces are broken up into small enough pieces, scoop them into a screw top jar or a tin with a lid. Always spoon out the pieces of glass that are to be fired in a pot and save lacerating your finger tips!

Containers: it is essential that all materials, dry and wet, are carefully stored in suitable closed containers and that they are clearly indelibly labelled, indicating the contents. Should you, by chance, be one of those teachers that has inherited a fascinating cupboard containing a selection of pottery ingredients in unmarked bags and jars that cannot be recognized by anybody in the school, please do not 'test' them out unless you are really experienced. Throw them away — better safe than sorry! Not very many years ago substances such as red lead, galena, lead carbonate, litharge and antimony oxide were regularly used. These chemicals are extremely dangerous so if you suspect you have anything of this calibre do seek advice from a specialist or from your local science adviser. If the ingredients are to be disposed of keep them under lock and key until this is done safely.

Hygiene and personal safety

(a) Working surfaces, tools and floors should be cleaned daily by washing and wet mopping. The use of domestic vacuum cleaners is inadequate to contain the dust. However, special sweeping compounds are available which are manufactured for this purpose. There are several varieties to suit different types of floors. (Names and addresses of suppliers will be found at the back of this book.)

(b) Personal hygiene is of utmost importance. Protective clothing (preferably of a nylon or terylene variety) should be provided, worn and regularly laundered.

(c) Always clean up a spillage as soon as it occurs — this applies to slurries as well as to powders because, when allowed to dry, a plastic clay or glaze slip becomes a source of dust.

(d) Packages of dry materials should be stored, opened and weighed in a suitably ventilated area and, ideally, the bags should be kept in lidded plastic containers or tins. Always ensure these containers are clearly labelled in an indelible ink.

(e) Eye protection: many potters are not aware of the damage that can be caused to eyes by peering through a spy hole into a hot kiln. Not only can the heat from the kiln damage the eye tissue and, even, the eyelashes and eyebrows, but also the brilliant light can harm the eyes if stared at for more than a second. Therefore if a kiln has to be peered into at this stage it is strongly recommended that sunglasses (not the plastic variety!) be worn or a piece of tinted glass is held in front of the spyhole before it is peered into.

First aid

A first aid kit should be kept visibly available in pottery areas and should contain disinfectant, burn cream, elastoplast, etc. Should anyone get anything lodged or splashed into the eyes, hold head over a bowl and splash liberally with cold water. Seek medical advice if in doubt.

EATING, SMOKING AND DRINKING IS PROHIBITED is a notice that should be displayed in pottery areas and observed! Hands should always be washed before leaving so that contamination is not passed onto food being consumed elsewhere.

Finally, I would suggest that when purchasing materials, teachers should refer to pottery suppliers' catalogues as most of them contain a lot of valuable information regarding safety and advice is always readily given regarding their individual products.

3 Kilns

Types of kiln

A kiln is as important to a potter as the clay itself, for without it he cannot make durable pottery.

Kilns come in a variety of types, shapes and sizes and much has been written on the subject already. Therefore, for the purpose of this book I intend to limit my comments to those most universally used in schools and endeavour to answer the questions most commonly put to me by teachers who feel that the kiln is an 'ogre' rather than a 'friend'.

Most schools nowadays possess some form of electric kiln although some secondary schools and colleges do have gas-fired kilns. Gas-fired kilns are far more flexible than electric kilns in as much as one can form a reducing atmosphere (ie a kiln atmosphere which is deficient in free oxygen and causes reduction of compounds rich in oxygen which may be present in it). However, though gas-fired kilns are cheaper to run they are very much more expensive to buy and so schools, being very conscious of capital outlay, tend to buy electric kilns.

Sizes of electric kilns used in schools very from the smallest with inside measures of 305 x 305 x 305 mm to the large-sized kiln 610 x 610 x 762 mm. A few schools may have smaller kilns and a few larger but this is the most common range for infant schools through to secondary schools and evening institutes. Prices of kilns vary quite considerably and I would recommend schools deciding to purchase a kiln to give serious consideration to those specifically designed for education purposes, eg the Hymus 'Essex' kilns. Most pottery suppliers list kilns in their catalogues and all these are good kilns, however consider price and muffle (inside) size before making a decision.

All kilns, irrespective of size, must comply with the safety regulations and, in some cases, the cost of updating a kiln to comply with these regulations can cost more than the kiln's original purchase price. However, considering present day prices it is still cheaper in most cases to service and update an old kiln than to buy new with all the added extras.

A partially packed kiln showing positioning of props

Kiln furniture and maintenance

Before discussing the practical use of a kiln ie the packing and firing, I shall look in more detail at the care, simple service and adjustments that concern a kiln and its aids:

(a) *Bats* (or shelves) — ensure that you have the correct sized bats. They should allow at least a 25 mm gap all round when placed inside the kiln. For example, if the muffle size of the kiln is 305 x 305 mm then the size of the bat should be no larger than 254 x 254. It is of the utmost importance to leave this gap in order to allow the hot air to circulate inside the kiln — otherwise the elements will quickly burn out! When new, bats should be coated with a bat wash (a combination of alumina and china clay or zircon and china clay) mixed to a thin paste with water. It is advisable to sprinkle silica

19

sand onto the bats as well, for the bat wash and silica sand together will protect the bats and help prevent pots sticking to them should the glaze run at a high temperature.

(b) *Bungs* — never push the firebrick bungs tightly into the vent or spy holes of a kiln. As the kiln heats up the bungs will expand and consequently be difficult to remove when cold — and possibly break. When inserting the bung, push it in and then withdraw it a fraction — this technique will usually solve the problem.

(c) *Props* — these are the spacing tubes that separate the shelves inside the kiln. Generally it is advisable to purchase the plain tubes as these do not chip and become damaged as easily as the castellated variety.

(d) *Cracks* — if cracks appear in the kiln and are fine ones, leave well alone as they are usually only expansion cracks. Should larger cracks appear it is advisable to wet the crack and then fill it with a fire cement. Slowly fire the kiln to around 400°C when dry, to set the cement.

(e) *Elements* — to extend the life of the elements in a kiln it is advisable to vary the temperatures of firings as much as is possible, eg after a stoneware firing, follow with a biscuit firing rather than repeat another stoneware firing. Do not touch the elements unless absolutely necessary as they become very brittle. Keep them clean by dusting away particles of dust and pottery with a soft brush. Should an element need to be replaced then follow the following instructions or call in an engineer:

1 Switch off the electricity supply to the kiln.

2 Remove the rear sheet metal cover.

3 Locate the element that has failed, loosen the corresponding connectors and withdraw the element from the front of the kiln.

4 Remove all cinder or burn marks from the element grooves. This is very important as if a metal deposit is left it may cause arcing. Repair any damage to brickwork with fire cement.

5 Fit new element into grooves and thread the element tails through the holes in the back wall.

6 Fit connectors onto the element tails. (It is helpful to have assistance at this stage — one person gently pushing the element from inside the kiln whilst the other works at the back.) Pull element tails with pliers whilst the connector screws are tightened.

7 Doublecheck that connector screws are tight. After the kiln has been fired four or five times, check the element tails for slackness. This often occurs due to expansion and this slackness must be taken up by loosening and retightening the connectors. If this is not done then arcing may occur and the elements burn out again very quickly at the tail ends.

8 It is advisable to fire the kiln once whilst empty, to around 1100°C, as this will enable the new element to acquire its protective oxide coating.

NB *Never* push mothballs into kilns in order to create a reducing atmosphere — the effects on your pottery might be interesting but your elements will be ruined!

(f) *Pyrometers* — if you already have a pyrometer and suspect its accuracy, check the dos and don'ts list given below and if all seems to be in order then it may need calibrating or lubricating. For this it will need to be sent back to the manufacturers or serviced by a specialist. The installation of a new pyrometer is quite critical if it is to perform accurately and the following checklist may be of help:

1 The indicator dial should be mounted on a vertical wall and it should sit

horizontally. It should be free from any form of vibration. It should not be subject to radiant heat, cold draughts or dampness.

2 Remove the shunt wire which is connected across the terminals at the back of the indicator dial. Its purpose is to protect the indicator in transit and it should always be replaced if the indicator is moved for any reason.

3 Never connect electric mains supply to the indicator terminals.

4 Check that the compensating cables do not run near to, or parallel to, electric mains cables — they should be at least 460 mm apart.

5 Don't use ordinary copper connecting cable — the cable provided is designed to compensate for temperature changes and other cables will not do so.

6 Never shorten or lengthen the cable or thermocouple as the indicator has been calibrated for a definite external resistance.

7 If in doubt, consult the manufacturer and don't try to do it yourself by opening the indicator where dust or fumes are in the atmosphere.

8 The thermocouple is usually quite easily pushed through a hole in the top of the kiln which has been drilled for the purpose. Some kilns do have the hole at the back of the kiln and occasionally there is no hole provided at all and one has to be drilled. However, provided the tip of the thermocouple projects into the firing chamber of the kiln and the indicator dial is mounted correctly, the pyrometer should give long and accurate service.

NB I would advise checking the accuracy of the dial readings with Staffordshire cones for the first two or three firings and if there is a slight variance this can usually be adjusted by means of the small adjusting screw at the base of the indicator dial — it is essential that this is done at *high* temperature.

Unpacking a kiln after a glaze firing. Note the position of the pyrometer on the wall

(g) *Kiln guards* — these can be purchased from various manufacturers but are quite expensive and it is not difficult to make one up oneself. To do this it is necessary to purchase the following: 5 or 6 lengths of 3 metre-long Dexion Slotted Angle 140 wire mesh, corner plates, 60 nuts and bolts, plastic feet. The guard can be made up as a two or three sided shape, as required, and pushed into position around the kiln when it is to be fired. This type of guard will satisfy the safety regulations and cost about one fifth of a proprietary guard.

Firing a kiln

1 New kilns: as these will not have been used before they must be 'broken in'. To do this switch to 'low' or about one third of the full temperature, with no pottery inside the kiln and ventilation bungs out. Leave the kiln on for about four or five hours. This will have a gentle drying out effect on the firebricks and cement which may still contain moisture from the time when the kiln was built. It will help the elements, of course, if you take the kiln up to around 1100°C whilst still empty in order to give them the protective coating as described earlier in this chapter. When this has been done your kiln is ready for use.

2 Packing a biscuit firing:

(a) Ensure that the pottery to be fired is absolutely *dry* — a rough guide is that it should not feel really cold to the touch and if a finger is rubbed over the surface then a fine powder should be deposited onto it.

(b) The pieces of pottery will not stick together in the kiln as there will be no glaze on them so pack them inside and on top of one another. However, take care not to wedge them tightly together and do leave gaps at the sides and at the top of the kiln as the pots will expand slightly before they start to shrink. Shrinkage at this stage is around one eighth. Place the larger and stronger pots at the bottom of the kiln and let them support the lighter ones. If there is really delicate pottery to be fired then use bats for support and separation.

(c) Commence the firing, with bungs out, slowly. I recommend that schools adopt the 'low overnight' process for all firings. In this way the clay is thoroughly dried out and if the kiln is taken up to its required temperature the next morning by putting in the bungs and switching up to high, a satisfactory firing will have been achieved with no aggravation. When the kiln has reached the required temperature of around 960°C switch the electricity off and allow the kiln to cool down slowly. Do not open the door until the next day, when it will be cold.

3 Packing a glaze firing:

(a) Check that any surplus glaze has been sponged off from the bottom of the pottery and about a quarter of an inch from the sides if the pottery is to be fired to stoneware temperature. Remember that any deposits of glaze will melt in the heat and cause the pottery to stick to the bats. Sprinkle the floor and bats with silica sand as this will help to prevent any overglazed ware sticking.

(b) Pack kiln with pieces of pottery so that they do not touch one another. If you push one pot up to another until it just touches and then withdraw it a fraction you will know it is not touching. Also it is wise to place pieces of similar height on the same shelf — this will economize on space. Arrange shelves and half shelves in such a way that the kiln will hold as much as possible. A full kiln will always produce a better firing than a half empty one. Remember to leave enough room for cones if they are to be used! It is important that the props supporting the shelves are placed directly above one another — use three props in a triangle in smaller kilns and five in larger kilns.

(c) Fire the kiln in the same way as for the biscuit firing, the only difference being that it will take longer for the kiln to reach the glaze fired temperature the next day, particularly if it is a 1260/80°C stoneware firing.

Firing schedule

Teachers will find the safest and easiest method of firing a kiln is to adopt the schedule mentioned above. *Always* place a notice above the kiln describing the type of firing and there will be less chance of things going wrong. Even if the person in charge of the kiln is away the following day it will be quite easy for a colleague to complete the firing without mishap. It is also useful to keep a firing log or chart as firing times are usually similar unless there is voltage reduction or surge. A typical example of firings might be:

Kiln on low	Kiln up high	Kiln turned off
Wed 4 pm Bung out	Thurs 9 am Bung In	11.35 am (960°C)
Wed 4 pm Bung out	Thurs 9 am Bung In	12.50 pm (1080°C)
Wed 4 pm Bung out	Thurs 9 am Bung In	2.45 pm (1260°C)

Measuring temperature

There are several methods for measuring the temperature inside a kiln and the most common of these used in schools are pyrometers and pyrometric cones. A pyrometer is a clock-type temperature indicator, usually calibrated 0-1400°C on an edgewise mirror scale. Pyrometric cones differ in as much as they determine the satisfactory completion of a firing. Their composition and structure is such that they bend when subjected to heat for a period of time, ie their operation is dependent on 'heat/work' and not temperature, though the end result is virtually the same, as the pottery is satisfactorily fired either way. Cones are graded according to the amount of heat work they withstand and are placed inside the kiln in alignment with the spy hole. There are many types of pottery, fired at many different temperatures but, in general, I would suggest that teachers use the following temperatures as a guide:

Type of firing	Temperature	Orton cone	Nearest staff. cone
Biscuit	960/980°C	07	06
Earthenware Glaze	1060/1080°C	04	02
Stoneware Glaze	1260/1280°C	9	9

NB I was interested to learn recently from a kiln manufacturer that when a kiln is switched off it does not immediately fall in temperature — it will, in fact, rise a few more degrees before falling. This is a fact that, I am sure, few teachers know.

Simple home-made outdoor kilns

Particular care is necessary when kilns of this type are used. These slow burning kilns must be adequately fenced and sited in safe places. Pupils should be warned of the dangers and a notice is advisable. It should be noted here that improvised equipment for oil or gas fired Raku kilns must not be used as all installations of this type need to be approved by a Fire Prevention Officer before use. The most popular outdoor kilns are clamp and sawdust:

1 *The clamp kiln:* dig a small pit in the ground (putting aside the turf) measuring about 610 mm across and 254-305 mm deep. Position three pieces of metal tubing (about 305-356 mm long) in triangular formation in the pit. Next, place some pieces of dry wood and some paper in the bottom of the pit and light it. When it is burning well, gently pile on some sawdust which will deaden the flames. Smoke should now been seen to be coming from the ventilation tubes, showing that the sawdust is smouldering. Embed the pots in the sawdust and cover them with more sawdust. Replace the turf over the mound and then place an old dustbin lid over the clamp in case it should rain. Leave the venting tubes open to the air. Smoke should issue from the tubes which are not facing the wind. When the fire has burned out, and this usually

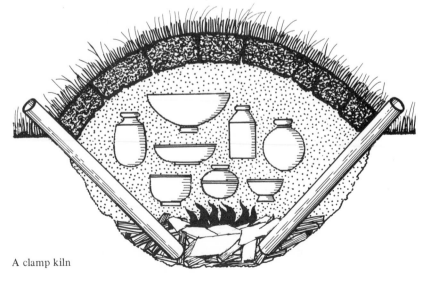

A clamp kiln

23

A sawdust kiln

takes between 12 and 16 hours, rake the pots out and you will be fascinated by the results.

2 *The sawdust kiln:* there are several ways of making a sawdust kiln and two of the most common methods are:

(a) A metal bin (eg a small dustbin) with a few holes punched in the sides, for ventilation, and lid on top.

(b) A cubic shaped brick built kiln using ordinary housebricks. Small gaps should be left between the bricks for ventilation and an old dustbin lid placed on top.

In both cases layer sawdust in the kiln, embedding the pots about 50-70 mm apart. Start the sawdust burning from the top by lighting a twisted piece of newspaper and placing the dustbin lid on top, slightly propped up. When the sawdust has finally smouldered away the firing is complete. This is likely to take between 16 and 24 hours — the longer the better!

Always allow kilns to cool completely before removing lid and unpacking — this will prevent unecessary cracking.

Tips: With all types of sawdust firing it is a good experiment to burnish the pots (preferably using terra cotta clay) with the back of a metal spoon handle, using a circular motion. This should be done at the leather hard stage. When really shiny allow them to dry completely before firing. The fired pots will have a lovely shiny finish — without glazing!

Should you be able to dig any local clay, this process of firing enables children to become involved in the complete process of making a pot and is very rewarding, particularly with younger children.

24

4 Clay

Types of clay

What is clay? In simple terms it is a product of the weathering of the earth's crust and as this weathering is continuous, clay forms a large part of that crust. Fortunately for potters it is an abundant material, although it can be a nuisance to farmers, miners and civil engineers. However, in ceramics its use is universal.

Before looking at the chemical differences and structures of various types of clay, let us look back to early times when man first recognized that this material, in its plastic state, could be worked and then allowed to harden. It is likely that animal footprints and tracks in clay soil which was hardened by the sun, first gave man the idea of using it.

Initially bricks were made and dried in the sun. Wicker baskets were able to be made water-proof by lining them with clay. In the Bible (Genesis 2,7) it says 'The Lord God formed man of dust from the ground'. Could this be a reference to clay? This question might make an interesting theme for a school assembly.

Whether the first hardening of clay by fire was intentional or accidental we cannot know but it is fascinating to note that fragments of pottery showing marks of wicker basket work have been found in the Nile Valley and it is estimated that these were made 13,000 years ago! In Britain the oldest pottery to be found is that which has been excavated from Roman times. The Romans made two types of pottery, a red variety called Samian ware and a black variety which is called Etruscan ware. A fact that interests and perplexes potters is that wherever in Europe Roman pottery has been found, the colour, texture and density are always the same — even though the Romans used local clays located at great distances from one another. There appears to be no obvious explanation for the similarity of all this pottery but it certainly creates an interesting subject for speculation.

Etruscan pot

The formation and classification of clay

Clay was initially formed thousands of years ago by the decomposition of feldspathic rocks. Rain, wind and frost continued the process of erosion, splitting the rock into ever smaller fragments. Some of these fragments were carried away by rivers and streams to places far away from their original beds and these much travelled clays are known as *secondary clays*. These clays have a varied composition because they tended to collect other materials in transit. If, for example, they came into contact with iron they turned red or yellow. Most red clays, ball clays and fireclays are classified as secondary clays. On the other hand, clays which are found in the place where they were formed, ie at their site of origin, are called *primary clays* or kaolin. In this country these clays are found largely in Cornwall and in addition to being used in pottery, kaolin or *china clay*, as it is most commonly known, is used widely by industry — for paint, medicines, cosmetics, paper and even car tyres.

25

Clay is indestructible: this statement applies to clays once they have been fired to high temperatures in a kiln. Chemical and physical changes occur during firing and the end product is as indestructible as natural rock. This is a very important fact which should be brought to the notice of all students and, in particular, to young children. It will encourage them to give only their best work to be fired, once they realize that what they make and fire will be there for posterity. Even if fired pottery is ground up or broken, it can never revert to its original clay state. Firing creates an irreversible change from 'clay' to 'pottery'.

Another method of classifying clays is their ability to fire to certain temperatures without distorting:

Refractory clays: the primary china clays come under this heading and some of the fireclays which are often coarse, but retain their shape and do not vitrify at very high temperatures. They are used for making high temperature kiln bricks and kiln furniture. Either of these clays can be added to other clays if temperatures of above 1260°C are needed.

Vitrifiable clays: with these clays the particles fuse together without loss of shape — hence good stoneware clays come into this category and, of course, porcelain.

Fusible clays: these are the lower-firing earthenware clays which lose their shape around 1200°C. They are clays which lie near to the surface and often contain large quantities of iron. They are used for bricks, tiles, etc. They are usually a reddish colour and are ideal for modelling.

The three main types of pottery are:

Earthenware: this can be fired from a lowest temperature of 700°C up to 1200°C which is the point of vitrification when deformation will commence. Earthenware is porous and requires glazing all over to make it non porous as the particles are not fused together.

Stoneware: 1200°C–1300°C — fired at these temperatures it is a hard material which is non porous and usually only requires glazing for hygienic and artistic reasons. The particles are fused and vitrified.

Porcelain: 1250°C–1400°C — very hard and non-porous. This type of clay is not very plastic, it is 'short' and hard to handle. It distorts easily but its real attraction is its whiteness and translucency if made thin enough.

Recommended types of clay

For school purposes I would recommend teachers to limit the types of clay they choose for reasons of facility and economy:

Primary Schools: a combination of a red terra-cotta clay and a grey general purpose clay. The red clay should fire to 1080°C and the grey clay to around 1260°C.
Senior Schools and Evening Class Groups: a selection of:

Red terra cotta clay, firing to earthenware temperatures

Grey stoneware clay,

A grogged stoneware clay
 (eg St Thomas's Body) } firing to stoneware temperatures

A crank type modelling clay

Should there be deposits of local clay that can be dug, it must be prepared before use. This can form a very interesting experiment and the following advice may well be of assistance in such a project:

26

Model showing the combination of red (hat) and grey clays

1 Having dug the clay or removed it from a river bank, break it into small pieces and remove any foreign objects such as stones or leaves. Ideally the clay should then be left to weather for a year or more but this is not really feasible in a teaching situation.

2 Put the clay into a bin and cover with water. Leave it for a few days, stirring it from time to time.

3 Brush the clay and water slurry through the coarsest sieve you can get (a garden sieve is good to start with) in order to remove more of the rubbish. Add more water as necessary and sieve through progressively smaller gauge sieves once the larger lumps have been reduced.

4 When slurry is smooth, spread it on a large plaster slab to dry. (A slab can easily be made using potters' plaster or even fine builders' plaster and setting it in a large tray.) Turn the clay from time to time as it dries.

5 Wedge and knead the clay when suitably plastic and store in polythene or airtight containers or bins.

6 It is advisable to do a firing test on the clay before spending time making objects with it. To do this fire to biscuit temperature (960°C) and check for shrinkage and warpage. Sometimes these faults can be corrected by the addition of a proprietary clay.

Most clays dug locally are fun but are rarely suitable for general use. Only experiment will show what the clay is best suited for.

Preparation of clay

All clay must be wedged and kneaded before use. This really is important and should be explained to pupils during the first clay lesson.

Wedging: take a large piece of clay and knock it into a block shape and cut it in half with a length of cutting wire or coarse fishing line. Throw one half down onto the other with as much force as possible. Repeat this process a number of times for it is this action that forces out the air pockets. Inspect the clay for air pockets each time you cut it.

27

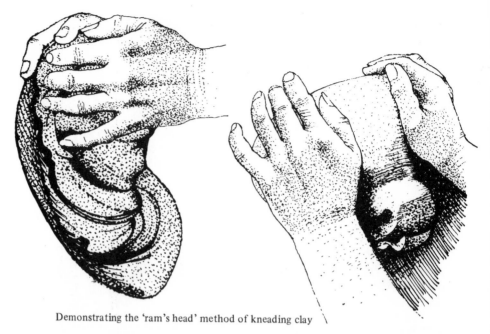

Demonstrating the 'ram's head' method of kneading clay

Kneading: there are several methods of kneading but I prefer the 'ram's head' method. This is done by taking a lump of wedged clay that you can comfortably handle with two hands and forcing the hands down with maximum pressure being exerted from the wrists. Lift the clay at the end farthest away from you and push forward onto it (the shape will resemble a ram's head, hence the name). Repeat the process several times and your clay will be kneaded. It is the same technique as the baker uses with his dough.

NB If clay is too soft it will firm up if kneaded on a plaster bat or on a wooden table top. However, should the clay be of correct consistency then it is best to wedge and knead the clay on a stone bench, as this will not absorb moisture from the clay.

Drying stages

It is useful to understand the various stages that clay passes through as it dries. Different techniques and uses can be made of clay at these various stages. Most clay must have water added to it to make it plastic (approximately one third of its dry weight is usual). As soon as a pot is made this water begins to evaporate from the surface of the pot and by capillary action from inside the clay mass. It is as the water between the clay particles dries that the particles draw together and cause shrinkage of the entire mass. The larger the grain size (relatively non-plastic clays) the less shrinkage takes place — hence the reason for the addition of sand or grog to reduce shrinkage. Because of shrinkage it is imperative that finished pots are dried evenly.

When drying green ware (ie unfired pottery) bear in mind the following factors:

(a) A large pot or a pot of uneven thickness needs very slow drying.

(b) Always avoid uneven drying such as placing a pot in a draught or allowing one side to be heated by sunlight or a radiator.

(c) Dry tiles slowly between bats and sheets of dampened newspaper.

(d) Take special care when drying pots with handles or spouts.

Remember uneven shrinkage will cause warpage or cracking. There are four basic stages that clay passes through as it dries:

(a) Liquid or slip state — this is the wettest; slip is used for decoration, casting and joining clay.

(b) The plastic state — this is the usual condition for making pottery — throwing, coiling, slabbing, modelling, etc.

(c) The leather hard or cheese hard state — at this stage pottery is turned on a wheel, handles and spouts are fixed. Slip decoration and burnishing may also be done at this stage.

(d) The dry state — the clay is now hard and brittle. Brush decoration is often done at this stage, using metal oxides and stains. All pottery must be in this condition before firing. It will not feel really cold to the touch and its colour will be lighter than its plastic state. It will also have a dusty surface.

Storage and recycling

Storage: clay should be stored in lidded bins. Suppliers usually pack clay in polythene which keeps it in good condition for a long time, provided the polythene is not punctured or torn. However, it is not practical to use the clay from the wrapper — far better to place it in a dustbin, or smaller bins, with airtight lids, can be bought for the purpose if preferred. A sheet of polythene placed under the lid will help keep the clay inside in good condition. In primary schools it is a good idea to have the clay balled up or cut up into small chunks before placing in the bin — this will save a lot of time at the beginning of a lesson. It is useful to have two bins for each type of clay used — one for the new clay and one for the used clay that will be recycled. Mark the bins clearly in such a way that the purpose of each bin is obvious, eg 'New red clay' and 'Used red clay.'

Recycling: in the 'Used' bin place all unfired clay that is too dry for ordinary use, ie all pieces of clay that have become dry due to exposure to room atmosphere and all reject pots that will not be fired. The only type of clay that must *never* be put back into the bins is that which is contaminated with foreign bodies, such as plaster. *Throw this away* as it will cause the clay to explode during firing or pieces of the pot to chip and flake off after firing. When sufficient clay has been collected in the used bin, cover it with water and leave for a couple of days, stirring it occasionally. Remove excess water and then spread it onto fairly thick plaster or wooden bats to dry. Turn it from time to time and wedge it before use. It can then be returned to the 'New clay' bin. In this way very little waste occurs.

Tired clay: clay can sometimes become 'tired' — just as we do! The reason for this is that it has been in constant use and the symptoms are that it will suddenly collapse, splitting as it folds. This is because the clay has been overworked and the cure is to leave it to rest, unused, for a week or so and then to mix it with some new clay before wedging and kneading it ready for use.

Pugmills: some secondary schools have pugmills and like to use them. This is really a matter of the teacher's personal preference. If using a pugmill feed the clay into it from the plaster bat, before it has become too dry. However, even after pugging, unless the pugmill is of a vertical sophisticated de-airing type, wedge and knead the clay before use.

It is important that after use, a pugmill is protected by placing a sheet of polythene over each aperture, unless the pugmill is to be dismantled completely and cleaned. This service is only necessary very occasionally or if the polythene protection has been forgotten and the clay inside has gone hard!

Tips

Damp cupboards: if you need a damp cupboard in which to store pots between making sessions and do not have enough money to buy a proprietary one, beg or borrow an old wooden or metal cupboard and line it with heavy duty polythene. Place a bowl of water at the bottom or a plaster bat soaked in water and you will have an excellent damp cupboard at very low cost — provided it is kept closed! Alternatively store pots in an ordinary cupboard or on shelves, but first wrap them securely in polythene bags, ensuring that they are airtight.

Use of grog: grog is finely ground pre-fired clay which, if added to clay by kneading it in, will reduce shrinkage and add strength whilst making. It will coarsen the surface texture and is ideal for slab pottery, model making and the throwing of large pots. By adding grog to clay the need for the hollowing out of models made by young children is not so crucial — as long as the drying process is observed.

Air drying clays

Mention should be made in this chapter of the new air-drying modelling clays that are now available from several suppliers. These are quite expensive to buy but for infant schools or small groups that do not possess a kiln, the world of working with clay is opened up instead of being a process which has to be denied. Objects made with this type of clay harden when exposed to the air. It is not a rapid process and so there is plenty of time for work to be carried out and drying can be retarded by covering the work with polythene. Left uncovered the finished work will become fully hard in two or three days. It can be decorated after half a day and when completely dry can be burnished or polished. A gloss finish and protection against moisture can be achieved by the application of a cold glaze which is usually supplied with the kit. All spare pieces of clay can be reconstituted, even when hard, if so desired. On the other hand, if a kiln becomes available pots made from this type of clay can be fired and glazed in exactly the same way as ordinary clays.

5 Oxides and stains

Mixing and application

Ceramic colours are known as metal oxides and they are finely ground to powder form so that they can be easily applied when mixed with a liquid. Usually they are mixed with water and applied to the pottery *before* it is biscuit fired. The usual form of appliction is to paint onto pottery using fine brushes. The best brushes for this purpose are Japanese brushes with long bristles, but these are expensive and should be washed carefully after use.

Some potters and books written on pottery suggest that ceramic colours should be applied to the biscuit fired ware. In many cases this technique, for various reasons, may be adopted by craft potters who control the use of their own glazes, but it is not a practical or economical method for use in schools. The reason that teachers are advised to paint the colours onto the raw clay and then biscuit fire before glazing is that in this way the glazes do not become contaminated by particles of oxides or stains which will wash off the pottery when dipped into the glaze bucket if not first fired into the clay. The only exception to this is if the oxides or stains are applied too thickly to the pottery — then no amount of firing will prevent the particles brushing or washing off.

In-glazing: this is an alternative form of applying colour to pottery and is the technique of applying oxides and stains over the unfired glaze — usually using a soft brush. The colours produced will be much brighter using this method but care should be taken not to damage the powdered surface of the glaze on the pot. Particular care should be taken of the rims of pots as if the glaze is knocked off it will leave a bare patch on the finished pot. The most suitable base glazes for this form of decoration are earthenware-temperature plain, opaque and transparent glazes. Sometimes the glazes will tend to change the colour of the oxide stain by lightening the shade and, in some cases, they will even change the colour completely, though this does not often happen with underglaze colours.

Colour oxides as sold by pottery suppliers form several categories which are:

(a) *Metal Oxides* — the most powerful form of colour — more powerful weight for weight than any other form of colour. Cobalt oxide is the most intense.

(b) *Metal Carbonates* — a less powerful form of colour.

(c) *Underglaze Colours* — are fully intermixable to permit a very wide range of colour possibilities. These colours are much less intense than are oxides and carbonates and, visually, look more like 'powder paints'. If fired to recommended glaze temperatures they will retain their original colours.

(d) *Glaze and Body Stains* — these can be added in quantities of 3%-10% to glazes or 5%-15% to slips and clay bodies. These stains can also be used as paints for direct application to an unfired glaze. These stains are usually inter-mixable.

Womble decorated with oxides and glazed (earthenware)

31

(e) *Onglaze Colours* — these are not widely used in schools — usually only at an advanced level. They need to be applied with skill and must be mixed with a liquid oil medium before applying to the fired glazed pot and then refired to temperatures varying between 730°C–800°C, according to the body used. They are usually applied using a brush or air-brush.

All oxides, carbonates and underglaze colours can be mixed with water for application and I recommend these be kept mixed in small quantities in screw capped jars as they do not deteriorate with use, provided *clean* brushes are always used. Should they dry up, just add more water — never throw away — these materials are much too expensive to buy in large quantities. Manganese dioxide and iron oxides are less expensive but others, particularly those containing cobalt or copper, are extremely expensive, so treat them with care.

NB Always label the jars containing colours as in some cases they are not always distinguishable from one another.

When painting onto pottery for best results it is advisable to paint thinly ensuring that the colour in the container is kept stirred — if the particles are allowed to drop to the bottom of the jar you will be applying only water from the top, or a much too thick mixture of colour from the bottom. It is important to remember that powdered metal is much heavier than water so will not stay in suspension for long. If it is painted on too thickly the resulting colour will be blackish and it will resist the glaze leaving the coloured area starved of glaze.

Test tile: it is very useful to make a test tile for some of the colouring oxides, showing the varying degrees of colour, according to the thickness applied. The colour that gives the greatest variety of shades is copper carbonate. To do this make a tile of grey clay 152 x 102 x 6 mm thick, and dry it slowly between two bats (so that it will dry flat and not curl up at the corners). When the tile is dry, paint stripes of copper carbonate (mixed with water) shading them from thinnest (palest) to thickest (brightest). Biscuit fire the tile, then glaze it with a white opaque glaze, firing to around 1060°C (Podmores P2116 is ideal for this). Most people are very surprised at the results — the stripes varying from palest green through beautiful rich greens to black. This is a good way of demonstrating the effects of a metal oxide. When applied really thickly a metal barrier is created between the clay and the glaze and consequently the glaze will not adhere — the result is a rather unpleasant blackish grey metallic colour. Allow pupils to be involved with these tests as they are a very important part of pottery education.

NB It is a good idea to make two holes in the tiles so that they may be hung up in the pottery area for all to see.

Storage of metallic oxides and stains

It is advisable to store these colours in containers with good seals such as screw top jars or plastic containers with firm clip-on lids. Do ensure that these containers are labelled *clearly* and *permanently*. It is very difficult to recognize the difference between some oxides — for example managanese dioxide, copper oxide, cobalt oxide and nickel; to the inexperienced eye, all look a similar shade of black. Unfortunately a lot of materials are wasted in schools because of loss of labels or their obliteration. It is wise, also, to mark the maker and catalogue number, eg copper carbonate — Podmores P3404.

Colours

I am often asked to suggest a list of colours for use in schools and to define the colours so I give below a basic list and the colours these oxides and stains will produce:

Most pottery suppliers stock the following colours but for an added reference I have given Podmores catalogue stock numbers.

Number	Colour	Colour produced
P3410	Iron Oxide Red	honey/rust red/dark brown
P3413	Iron Oxide Yellow Ochre	yellow — brown
P3415	Manganese Dioxide	light brown/purple/black
P3404	Copper Carbonate	light/green/green/black
P3414	Manganese Carbonate	pink — browns
P4455	Turquoise Blue Underglaze Colour	light blue/green
P4459	Mazarine Blue	rich blue/royal blue
P4465	Amber Orange	yellow — gold
P4476	White	creamy white
P4475	Black	jet black

Crayons: for younger children in primary schools the lead free underglaze crayons are most useful (P4430). They are used like chalks and may be used on the biscuit surface or on the unfired greenware. They are sold in sets of ten colours which are: light green, dark green, light blue, dark blue, brown, sepia brown, pink, orange, yellow and black.

NB All the above colours will fire up to a temperature of 1280°C.

Pinch pot, shaped like a rose, decorated with oxide (copper) and a white stoneware glaze

33

6 Slips

Slip is a suspension of clay in water, and is made by mixing clay (usually dry) and water in about equal proportions. Slips have several uses and amongst these are casting, decorating and joining pieces of clay together.

Joining

The most common use of slip is for joining two pieces of clay, eg handles to pots, two slabs of clay, or limbs to models. The slip, in this case, is simply made up from the clay body being used, mixed with water to make a thin paste and then used like a 'glue' to join the two roughened surfaces together.

Slip decoration

For this purpose the slips need to be of a consistency similar to that of double cream and a good recipe for a general purpose decorating slip is:

1 kg ball clay – powdered
1 kg china clay – powdered
2¼ litres of water
1 tsp bentonite

This makes a white slip. Mix well and sieve through an 80 mesh sieve and store in a screw top plastic bottle. This is easy to shake before use. Alternatively, soak down some of the same clay as used for making pots and stain it to produce different coloured slips. The colours, however, must be darker than the clay itself. For lighter colours use white slip as a base.

Students applying slip as a form of decoration

Coloured slips

To make these add powdered oxides or stains to the dry ingredients. The amount of colour depends on individual requirements and must be according to experimentation. However, it is a good idea to make up a quantity of white slip as suggested above, then divide it into four or five equal portions, putting aside a white portion. Mix the other three portions, each with different colours and resieve. In this way you will have four or five different coloured slips to experiment with. To start with try adding two dsp of iron oxide (red) and one dsp of manganese dioxide – this should give a pleasant dark brown slip. A dsp of copper carbonate should give a pleasant green slip and a tbsp of blue stain will give blue slip. The recommended proportions are between 2½% and 10% according to the strength of colour required.

NB The bentonite is added to prevent the clay mass settling into a solid state at the bottom of the bucket or plastic bottle after it has been left unstirred for a while.

Various techniques of slip decoration are described in Chapter 8. However, it is important to note that slips should be applied to pottery while it is in its

Slip decorated dishes —
feathered

green stage and before it becomes fully cheese hard — this is to prevent the difference in contraction or shrinkage whilst drying.

Slip casting

This technique is great fun but best done with small groups. When mixing a casting slip make a fairly large quantity as it will keep for a long period if not used.

Recipe
4½ kg china clay
4½kg ball clay
4 litres of water
28g silicate of soda or mangers water glass
28g soda ash or washing soda.

Dissolve the silicate of soda in a little very hot water and add the soda. Then mix with the water. When dissolved sprinkle the clay into the water, stirring all the time. (It is advisable to wear a mask during this process). When mixed, brush through an 80 mesh sieve — preferably twice — and leave to stand for a day or so before use. The sodas act as a deflocculent and keep the clay in suspension, as well as making it more fluid. If on the next occasion you find the slip too thick, add more water, mix and sieve. On the other hand if the slip is too thin, having allowed it to stand, remove some of the surplus water that is resting on top of the slurry by gently pouring or syphoning it off — then stir and resieve. Remember it is always easier to thin than to thicken! For the casting, have the moulds ready — ie clean and dry with any joins sealed with clay to prevent leakage. Plaster moulds can be bought from most pottery suppliers or can be made very cheaply in the studio, workshop or classroom. Follow the procedure outlined below:

1 Check mould is bone dry and in good condition.

2 Check there are no leaky gaps if the mould is one with several pieces; if so seal with clay.

3 Pour slip gently into the mould.

4 Top up with more slip as the level of the slip lowers in the mould. The plaster absorbs water from the slip leaving the clay to form and thicken.

5 Watch the thickening process and time it. When the wall of the pot is the thickness you require (not less than 3 mm thick) pour out the surplus slip and return mould to its upright position to prevent bubbles forming on the base of the pot. Casting earthenware takes 20-30 minutes in a dry mould.

6 When the pot has dried to a cheese hard state it should then be removed from the mould. This drying process will take two to three hours and during this time the clay form will shrink away from the plaster mould. It is advisable to time this process from beginning to end for every time a really dry

mould is used the timing should be the same — that is, of course, provided the consistency of the slip is correct.

7 Any further trimming with a knife or sponging of the pot — particularly around the seams — should be done when the pot is quite hard and not liable to be distorted by handling. The technical term for sponging a pot at this stage is 'fettling'.

Making a simple plaster mould

1 Obtain an ordinary plastic washing-up bowl.

2 Make a solid mound of clay (eg shaped like a simple oval dish upside down) and smooth well with a fine sponge.

3 Place mound of clay, flat side down, on the bottom of the plastic bowl.

4 Take another bowl and fill one third full with cold water. Sprinkle into this some plaster of paris and keep doing so until you see peaks of plaster above the water line. *Do not stir* during this process. When the peaks of plaster show above the water and remain, stir well. A guide to quantity is 2 kg plaster of paris to 1½ litres of water and remember *always* add plaster to water.

5 Pour the plaster of paris into the plastic bowl over the clay mound. Gently pat the surface for bubbles and leave for 20-30 minutes.

6 Whilst waiting for the plaster to set, wash the plaster mixing bowl with running cold water and leave the tap running for several minutes to ensure the drains are clear of plaster particles — otherwise drains can block!

7 During this time the plaster of paris will 'heat up' and become solid. When it is set manipulate the plastic bowl so that the plaster mould falls free. Be careful not to let it drop! Turn it over and remove the clay mound from the plaster mould using a wooden or plastic spatula. Then smooth off any sharp edges with a wooden stick or light scourer. Wash mould and leave it to dry in a warm place for a day or so until it is completely dry.

Result: You will have made a mould that will produce many replica shapes, but remember *never* use a metal knife to trim the clay in a plaster mould. Always use a plastic spatula or a wooden stick and moulds will not be damaged nor will particles of plaster get embedded into the clay pot.
NB Always sponge plaster moulds with a damp sponge before use — this will prevent pinholing.

If clay becomes contaminated with plaster it must be thrown away or kept quite separately to be used *only* for mould making. Plaster in clay causes minor explosions during firing or pieces of pottery to chip off at a later stage.

Moulds may also be made by pouring plaster of paris over simple commercially made items, eg bowls, plates, etc. However, it is necessary to coat these objects, initially, with a solution made from soft green soap dissolved in boiling water (ratio 113g to 142ml water) This should be applied with a small sponge. Alternatively, a mouldmaker's size can be purchased from pottery suppliers, especially for this purpose.

Hump moulds: these are convex moulds and cannot be used with slip. Plastic clay must be rolled out, draped over the hump mould and trimmed with a spatula. If left for approximately 20 minutes in a dry, warm atmosphere the mould and clay should part company fairly easily. It is important to note that clay must not be left on a hump mould for longer than is necessary as the clay will shrink as it dries and consequently the form will crack or split. Dishes made by this method are, of course, ideal for slip decoration.

7 Glazes

Many books have been written on the intricacies and the chemistry of pottery glazes. However, in this chapter my aim is only to give brief guidelines that will enable teachers to formulate a simple understanding of the practical application of glazes and so provide pupils with successfully glazed pottery.

Most students will ask the obvious question 'What is a glaze?' The answer is that glaze is a form of glass. Basically there is no difference between a glaze and glass except that glass is melted first, and the shapes formed in the molten state, whereas a glaze is melted on a shaped clay surface, the biscuit fired pot. Bernard Leach says of glazes: 'as clothes are to the human body so are glazes to pots'. They are made from a variety of clay-based powders and oxides and the end product ie the colour, surface, texture and feel, will vary according to the recipes used and indeed from batch to batch with the same recipe. I have heard glazes compared to wine in as much as although they are basically quite simple they do depend upon the subtle quality of their ingredients which may vary according to their source and age.

The purpose of a glaze is to make pottery non-porous, resistant to scratching and to create certain decorative effects. It should be useful *and* visually attractive.

Most schools nowadays purchase ready made glazes and in this way they reduce the complication of having to use many different firing temperatures and also save a lot of time and trouble obtaining and mixing a large variety of raw materials. However, there are a few stoneware glazes, particularly ash glazes, that are fun to mix and experiment with and I will give a few recipes at the end of this chapter. It is generally considered wise to buy glazes from the same manufacturer as you buy your clay from because if the glaze is designed to go with the clay then there will be no problems in making the glaze fit the ware and simple faults like crazing and peeling are less likely to occur.

Two types of glaze are normally used in schools, ie earthenware glazes, which fire to around 1080°C and appear to lie on the surface of the pot, and stoneware glazes which fire to around 1260°C and actually fuse into the body of the pot. Reference is sometimes made to raw glazing — this is when glaze is applied to a green pot, (at the leather hard stage) dried and then fired to the temperature of the glaze. Ignoring the biscuit stage can cause many problems and therefore raw glazing is not normally recommended in schools — however, it can be fun to experiment with!

Coloured glazes

A simple method of acquiring a variety of coloured glazes from base glazes is to add oxides to such glazes as transparent and white opaque earthenware glazes. A rough guide as to how much colour to add is as follows:

black	10% manganese dioxide
white	5%-10% tin oxide

Thumb pot with coiled neck
decorated with two glazes

blue	½% cobalt carbonate
	or 1%-5% blue stain
green	2% copper carbonate
light brown	2% iron oxide
brown	4% iron oxide
	or 2% iron oxide and 2% manganese dioxide
grey	2% iron chromate

Combinations of oxides can be used but experiment first with small quantities for they do not blend like paints and sometimes the results can be quite surprising.

NB It is a very good idea to keep a glaze recipe book showing the firing temperatures, times and recipes for each glaze. Record the results also and you will find that such a book will become invaluable over the years — especially if you wish to repeat a particularly successful venture.

Test tiles or rings; another recording method, which is fun to make and there for all to see, is to make a set of small biscuit fired tiles which can be dipped into the various glazes and glaze fired. These can then be set up in a pattern on a frame forming a picture with a written description of the individual glazes underneath. Alternatively, rings can be made by rolling out a piece of clay, joining the ends to form a ring and flattening one side so it will stand up (like a serviette ring). Write the name of the glaze with a brush dipped in a dark oxide, on the underside of the ring. The advantage of these rings is that they have a vertical face which will demonstrate how a glaze runs. However, do remember to mark each experiment clearly or it becomes a pointless exercise.

Mixing

All glazes are mixed in the same way — that is unless the manufacturer specifically suggests an alternative method, as sometimes occurs with crystalline glazes.

You will need: a 10 litre bucket and lid, a large mixing bowl or another bucket, a glaze mop (large brush), 80 mesh sieve, 120 mesh sieve, 2 slats 457 mm long, bentonite, glaze powder, water, *and* a paper mask or a scarf tied around your nose and mouth.

NB If you do not have a glaze mop, tie a dozen large classroom type paintbrushes together.

(a) Two thirds fill the bucket with water — preferably warm.

(b) Add to water about 4 kg of glaze powder and 1%-2% by weight of bentonite (approx 1 dsp) and mix in.

(c) Place the two slats over the bowl or second bucket and set the 80 mesh sieve on the slats.

(d) Pour the glaze and water mixture through the sieve, brushing in a circular motion all the time.

(e) Replace the slats over the original bucket and set the 120 mesh sieve on the slats.

(f) Pour the once-sieved glaze through the 120 sieve, brushing in a circular motion once again.

(g) The glaze is now mixed so *label bucket clearly*, eg white opaque glaze P2116 (E)

(h) Leave to stand for several hours — preferably until next day.

Tips:

(a) *Always* label buckets and mark (S) for stoneware or (E) for earthenware. This indicates the temperature range at which the glazes are to be fired.

(b) Always add bentonite as this is a suspender and prevents the glaze sticking firmly to the bottom of the bucket when it has been left to settle.

(c) A *rough* guide for mixing a glaze is 800g glaze powder to 1 litre of water.

Consistency of a glaze

Before applying a glaze always check its consistency and adjust according to your requirements

(a) Assess the biscuit state of the pots to be glazed, ie if they have been fired to around 960°C then a normal single cream consistency will be required. However, if the pots have been underfired then the glaze will need to be thinner than normal as the pottery will be more porous. Conversely, should the pots have been overfired at the biscuit stage (ie over 1000°C) then the glaze will need to be thicker than normal as the clay will have begun to vitrify. It always helps in such cases to heat the pots in the kiln to around 100°C before applying the glaze as the heating up process will open up the pores and make the pots more porous and the glaze easier to apply.

(b) Test the glaze by pouring off about a pint of the still water resting on the top of the glaze in the bucket into a jar or bowl. Then stir the glaze well. Normally it will be fairly thick at this stage but dip a *dry* finger into the glaze and see how it coats your finger. It should have a smooth coating similar to that of single cream. If it is thicker than is required then pour some of the original water back into the glaze bucket, testing as you do it — but do remember *always* use a dry finger. Bearing in mind the variations in consistency according to the biscuit temperatures of the pots proceed as below.

Tip: before applying the glaze check that the pots are not dusty. It is a good idea to sponge pottery over with a slightly damp sponge before glazing — this will prevent the dust particles resting on the surface of the pottery and so causing pinholes and tiny bubbles which will inhibit the smooth overall glazing process of the pottery.

Glaze application

There are several methods of applying glaze to biscuit fire pottery and some of them are listed below:

(a) *Dipping and Pouring:* if the inside of a pot needs glazing, do this first by pouring some glaze from a jug into the pot, filling it to the brim and turning it as you pour it out again. Then hold the pot by its base and dip it into the bucket, holding it there for approximately 4-5 seconds. Remove slowly and hold still for a few seconds in the inverted position so that the drips will fall down back into the bucket and not down the side of the pot. Then place the pot onto a piece of newspaper. When dry (and this only takes a few seconds) clean off any glaze that has splashed onto the bottom of the pot using a wet sponge — hold the pot upright as you do this to prevent any water trickling down over the fresh glaze on the pot. The glazed pot may be handled provided your fingers are dry and you use a firm grip taking care not to rub off the fresh glaze. If glaze is rubbed off at this stage it will leave a bare patch when fired, so particular care needs to be taken of rims and handles or any place on a model or pot that has sharp edges.

(b) *Pouring* (only); this method is used usually for awkward shaped models or sculptural forms, or when there is only a small quantity of glaze available. Proceed in the same way as explained in the paragraph above on dipping and pouring. However, instead of dipping the pot into the bucket, either hold the pot in one hand and pour glaze on to it from a jug held in the other hand whilst rotating the pot or, place the pot on two slats over the bucket and pour the glaze over it, catching the surplus glaze in the bucket beneath.

(c) *Brushing:* glaze can be applied with a brush but it is not really recommended for general use as the effects can be patchy and streaky. It is, however, a very useful technique for touching up models with odd crevices that get missed with the pouring or dipping methods, or for touching up a bare spot that has been covered by the finger tips.

(d) *A second glaze:* double dipping, pouring or brushing a second glaze of a different colour over the first glaze can be very effective. A second glaze can also look well if splashed on. Remember that the second glaze should be slightly thinner than that used for the first application. Stoneware glazes react particularly well with this technique.

(e) *Spraying:* this technique is only recommended for senior schools and adult education. Expensive equipment is required: a spray booth, which must be ducted through a wall or which has permanent filters, and a compressor and spray gun with various nozzles. The final effect is a very even glaze and the saving is in the quantity of glaze used — for spraying will usually coat the pottery much more thinly. Before purchasing a spray booth it is wise to seek advice from the manufacturer and, if possible, have a demonstration of the equipment to be purchased. It is a very expensive item and it can be wasted if not used correctly. Generally, when spraying, the glaze is mixed to a thinner consistency than for dipping or pouring.

Firing

As soon as the glaze is dry the pots may be packed into the kiln and fired. When doing this make sure that no two pots touch each other and check that all the bases of the pots are free from glaze. At higher temperatures glazes become molten and sticky and so pots that are touching will stick together on cooling. A good method for checking that pots do not touch is to place the first pot in the kiln, then move the next up to it until you feel it touch and then move it away a fraction. In this way valuable kiln space is not wasted and you can be certain that the pots are not touching. It is necessary always to check the firing temperature recommended by the manufacturer of a glaze and it is best not to mix firing temperatures of different glazes if accurate results are expected. Never open the kiln door until the kiln is cold. It is extremely tempting to have a peep in the latter stages of the cooling process but if a draught is introduced into the kiln crazing will sometimes occur which is a great pity after all the weeks of hard work and waiting.

Tips

(a) An important point to remember is that the glaze in the bucket should be kept constantly stirred as glaze particles which are insoluble are heavier than water and will tend to drop to the bottom of the bucket. Very often

Contrasting glazes – black and white figures (earthenware)

'starved' pottery is due to this omission. The glaze mixture in the bucket may be perfect but if it is not kept stirred the vital particles of glaze needed to complete the process will never reach the pot.

(b) Remember that if a large quantity of pottery is to be glazed at one time, it will be necessary to check the consistency of the glaze periodically and sometimes extra water may need to be added. The reason for this is that porous pottery removes more water than glaze particles with the result that the glaze in the bucket will become thicker as more pots are glazed. When a piece of pottery is dipped into a glaze the water is absorbed into the biscuit fired clay leaving a coating of glaze on the outside and this, when fired, creates the glaze (or glass) layer. The water in the glaze bucket is only there to facilitate the application of the powdered glaze to the pottery.

(c) Should a pot become really messy during the glazing process – for example if it is inadvertently dropped into the bucket or too much glaze is poured onto it, it can be washed off. Endeavour to collect the washed off glaze as it can be returned to the bucket. When the pot is clean again it should then be re-fired to biscuit temperature before re-glazing. If in a hurry it is sometimes possible just to re-heat the pot and glaze it whilst it is hot. Glaze sticks much more readily to a hot pot than to a cold one.

(d) Generally leave a rim of approximately 3 mm clear of glaze at the base of a pot – this will allow for any glaze that might run down or even 'stretch'.

(e) When attempting to re-glaze over a pre-fired glaze ensure the glaze to be applied is really thick (at least double cream consistency) and always warm the pot before glazing.

(f) When a bucket of mixed glaze has been left for a long time the water may have evaporated. In such a case do not throw the solid mass away as it can easily be reconstituted. Just break up the mass at the bottom of the bucket, add fresh water and sieve. It will be ready for use again in the same way as a newly mixed glaze.

41

Ordering glazes

For the teacher faced, for the first time, by an array of pottery catalogues and the task of ordering some glazes, it is often very confusing and difficult to know where to start. I give below a few suggestions that have proved to be good base glazes. These are particularly suitable for primary schools with small kilns and fire at a temperature of around 1060/1080°C.

White opaque glaze

A vellum type opaque glaze is pearly smooth to the touch and is, in my opinion, one of the most useful glazes of all. Colours may be added to it to form coloured opaque glazes and it also blends well with a coloured transparent glaze which can be applied over it. Should it be desirable to convert an opaque glaze (which has a shiny finish) into a matt glaze, add 18 parts of zinc oxide and 4 parts of titanium dioxide and cool the kiln slowly. My preference for a white opaque glaze is Podmore's P2116.

Transparent glaze

This is not an expensive glaze and is very useful to use purely as a transparent glass covering for pottery or for mixing with colours to form coloured transparent glazes. I suggest a glaze similar to Podmore's P2106 and 5 kg is plenty to start with.

Honey glaze

This is extremely effective over red clay as it produces a deep rich shiny honey colour. Podmore's P2140 is an excellent choice

The above glazes are all fired at earthenware temperatures. However, in the stoneware range of glazes the choice is very wide indeed and it, therefore, tends to be a matter for personal choice. It is best to start off with about four basic glazes which will fire at around 1260°C–1280°C, examples being:

(a) Oatmeal (matt): this is a very useful glaze, looking well on thrown ware and on hand built pottery. It has a very professional appearance. Wengers 1604W is an excellent choice.

(b) A creamy white stoneware glaze is particularly useful when used as a base glaze with another glaze being dribbled over it or when an oxide decoration is applied beneath it. Wengers 1602W (Bristol) and Podmores P2313 (Sculptors' Glaze) are very suitable.

(c) A tenmoku glaze is a favourite of most potters. It is a classical Japanese glaze which has lovely variations from light browns through to the darker browns and black. It is normally shiny, unless underfired. As it reacts best to a high stoneware temperature it is best to place pottery glazed in tenmoku at the top of the kiln. It reacts very well over red slips.

(d) A coloured stoneware glaze – there are of course very many to choose from but I would suggest that initially one from the blue range of colours is very practical. Wengers blue grey, 1611W, is a good example, being useful as a straight glaze as well as extremely effective if used as a second glaze and dribbled over a light base glaze such as the Bristol. Very interesting effects can be created with this glaze if parts are rubbed off after glazing and before firing. The colours it will produce vary between a golden brown, where thinly applied or rubbed, to a rich greenish turquoise where it is applied thickly.

The glazes suggested above are intended purely as a guide for those embarking on a stock of stoneware glazes for the first time. As time goes by and funds improve the need will almost certainly arise for a wider variety of glazes so add to your stock gradually — remember it is the particular choice of glazes and the way they are applied that creates the individual characteristics of each person's pottery.

Simple recipes

To mix one's own glaze is a very satisfying experience but should not be attempted by those who are untrained or inexperienced in the handling of glazes. However, I give below a few simple stoneware glaze recipes for those who feel they are ready to attempt their own glaze mixing:

1 *White matt stoneware glaze* — firing temperature 1250°C—1260°C

Parts
20 feldspar
27 nepheline syenite
23 cornish stone
18 whiting
12 china clay
6 titanium

Looks very well over copper carbonate underglaze decoration.

2 *Iron brown glaze* — firing temperature 1250°C—1260°C

Parts
33 feldspar
22 whiting
35 china clay
10 quartz
5 iron oxide

Good on thrownware.
Good if diluted
and then double dipped.

3 *Turquoise stoneware glaze*
— firing temperature 1250°C—1280°C

Parts
39 feldspar
26 flint
5 china clay
11 whiting
6 colemanite
3 magnesium carbonate
9 barium carbonate
½ cobalt carbonate
1 chromium oxide.

Coiled pot splashed with a contrasting glaze

Ash glazes

These are, perhaps, the most interesting to make and experiment with for they are the most variable. Ash obtained from burning different woods will vary according to many factors such as the type of wood, the soil it grows in and the season. When the ash has been collected it must be sieved to remove charcoal pieces and then sometimes it is washed to remove soluble materials (this is a matter of choice and it is interesting to use it in two batches — washed and unwashed). When handling ash mixed with water always use rubber gloves as wet ash is often slightly caustic and may cause skin irritation.

43

As the ash is slightly soluble in the glaze it is best mixed and used at once. Throw away all the mixed glaze that is not used as it will deteriorate quickly. Some simple ash glaze recipes are given below:

50 parts wood ash
50 parts china clay   Fire to 1250°C and apply fairly thickly

NB Sieve 80 mesh only. The addition of ½%-3% of colouring oxides give a wide variety of colours.

The following ash glaze recipe will fire between 1200°C–1250°C

Parts
50   feldspar potash
10   china clay
10   whiting
30   wood ash

NB Sieve 80 mesh only.

Obviously there is plenty of opportunity for experiment with these glazes as different woods create different colours in the form of ash glazes and the fluxing (melting) properties also vary. Such glazes are fascinating to make but do keep recipe notes as it is most infuriating to create a lovely glaze and not to be able to repeat it at a later date.

Summary of firing temperatures:

(a) Majolica glazes (low temperature) 900°C–1050°C (same range as biscuit ware.)
(b) Earthenware glazes 1000°C–1150°C
(c) Stoneware glazes 1200°C–1300°C
(d) Porcelain glazes 1300°C upwards.

NB If glazes should become contaminated by colours do not throw away but keep as a base glaze and add a darker colourant. In this way an extra glaze will be added to your stock. These mixed up remnants of glazes are often ideal fo sculptural models.

8 Decorating techniques

There are many ways to decorate a pot and tremendous satisfaction can be had by exploring some of the techniques available to the potter who thinks. It is very important that the chosen form of decoration should suit the pot. Naturally an aesthetic awareness comes with years of experience but much can be gained by looking at and analyzing the work of the craftsmen potters. There are books containing beautiful photographs of pottery and, of course, exhibitions to be visited where close-up studies may be made. Perhaps one of the best guidelines is to remember that as a picture frame should enhance a picture so the decoration of a pot should seem to belong to it and suit its shape. Due to the fact that hand-built pottery is usually fairly robust it is inadvisable to aim for really delicate decoration, eg fine writing and the painting of pictures do not generally turn out very successfully and this form of decoration is, therefore, best avoided.

Below I explain the methods of decoration that I have found to be most successful:

Coloured clays

(a) *Mixing colours:* some very interesting and unexpected patterns can be created by the use of two or three different coloured clays mixed together by kneading before making the pot. Coloured clays can be obtained by mixing oxides or body stains into slip (2%-8% according to the strength of colour required) and then allowing the slip to dry to a plastic clay state. Always knead well before use.

(b) *Red and grey clays:* if you have these two common clays, as in most schools, some very interesting effects can be created by just using each clay individually whilst building a pot. For example, a house could be built with red brick walls and a grey roof and door. Remember, however, to glaze and fire such pottery to the temperature of the clay of the lowest optimum — this is usually in the earthenware temperature range.

Slips

These can be made up quite simply by adding the required amount of colour to white slip and sieving through an 80 mesh sieve. The slip needs to be of a consistency equal to that of double cream. It can then be applied in a variety of ways. (NB Slip must *always* be applied to pottery whilst it is in its 'green' condition, ie never to clay harder than the leather hard stage.)

(a) *Painting* — it is wise to paint the outline onto a pot first with powder paint or to use a stencil. Then paint the slip onto the pot boldly, over the powder paint which will fire away leaving a clear slip outline. Impressions made in a clay surface often look well when painted with coloured slips. Any surplus or smudged slip may be scraped off leaving a clean finish.

(b) *Slip trailing* — before attempting this, decide on the pattern to be adopted and make a powder paint outline if necessary. Fill a slip trailer (be it an orthodox bulb type slip trailer or a hairdresser's applicator bottle) with a thick coloured slip. Hold the nozzle of the trailer just above the surface of the clay and squeeze gently, drawing the nozzle firmly in the required direction. It is advisable to test the trail line on a piece of paper first in order to check the regularity of the flow.

(c) *Resist* — this form of decoration can be done in several ways, eg using wax resist (for school use best purchased in solution form) which is painted onto the leather hard pot which in turn, is then dipped into the coloured slip. This will not stick to the wax surface and consequently the pattern is left bare. Alternatively, pieces of dampened newspaper or wet leaves may be stuck to the pot and sponged over and dipped into the slip. Several hours later when the slip has lost its shine and is therefore dry the paper of leaves may be lifted off carefully with a pin. Several different coloured layers can be added in stages using this technique, but it is important to ensure that each layer of slip is set before adding the next. After biscuit firing this type of decoration usually only requires to be glazed in a transparent glaze. Paper doilies make excellent resist patterns for tiles and plates.

(d) *Sgraffito* — The term is Italian and it means 'scratched'. It is an interesting form of decoration and consists of scratching away at a pot which has been dipped into a slip. The scratching reveals the colour of the clay underneath, but care must be taken as mistakes cannot easily be rectified. Sgraffito is particularly effective on tiles and here, again, a stencil can be very useful.

(e) *Marbling and feathering* — marbling is great fun; it is simple and can be successfully applied by even the youngest potter. For example, make a tile of clay and coat it with a coloured slip — pouring or dipping. Next take a slip trailer containing another coloured slip and dot some slip onto the first coating whilst still wet. Swirl tile around and a pretty marbled effect will be formed. This technique is very effective when applied to press moulded or slip moulded dishes and bowls — whilst still in the mould. For these use the same technique as for the tiles, coating the inside of the dish and pouring off the excess slip before applying the second colour and swirling around. Leave the dish and slip to dry before removing the dish from its mould. For feathering, instead of dotting the second colour over the slip coating, trail several lines across the surface and then with a feather or a bristle draw lines through the slips in the opposite direction. This will cause drag marks which will form an attractive pattern. There are many variations on this theme and experimentating can be great fun.

NB Opaque glazes can be used over coloured slips but the effects tend to be muted so I recommend the transparent varieties.

Other techniques

Whilst still thinking of ideas to decorate pottery in its green state let us consider such methods as texturing, incising, inlay, applied and stamped ornamentation.

(a) *Texturing* — many interesting clay textures can be created from a wide variety of objects. Sometimes these objects can be pressed into, or dragged over, the finished pot and sometimes it is better to texture the clay whilst in its initial plastic state, allowing it to dry slightly before carefully making it into its 'pot' shape, eg slab pots. Articles that could usefully be added to a box of texture aids might well include some of the following: bark, broken brick, rough string, polystyrene tile pieces, wire mesh, hair rollers, carved furniture casters, springs, buttons, corrugated paper rolled up, broken pieces of wood, odd stones, etc. And remember that your own finger tips can often be your best tools — make imprints and try dragging them as they press into the soft clay then pinch and twist. Also, collect a variety of different textured materials, such as hessians, as these create effective textures when clay is rolled out over them.

Bottle textured by rolling clay over bark of a tree before making

(b) *Incising* — using a V-shaped lino-cutting tool patterns can be incised into the surface of the pot and if the cuts are well pronounced these cuts will show up clearly and not disappear under a coating of glaze. Oxides can be effectively rubbed into these cuts and the surplus dusted off.

(c) *Inlay* — cuts made with a lino cutting tool can be filled with clay or slip of another colour. The surplus can easily be removed with a metal scraper. When adding plastic clay it sometimes helps to brush water or slip into the cuts to help the clay stick.

(d) *Applied ornamentation* — small pieces or strips of clay may be added in the form of a decoration to pots whilst still at the leather-hard stage. To do this the pot must be roughened where the pieces are to go and then the pieces or strips should be stuck on with slip. It is important that the piece of clay to be applied is in the same state as the pot itself — if not the added pieces will drop off as the pot dries.

(e) *Sprigging* — this is another form of applied decoration and can be done by making a small mould of plaster of paris and casting a suitable motif — it is a similar process to that used for large moulds. Alternatively a motif can be carved into a piece of plaster, this can then be filled with slip or plastic clay can be pressed into it. Surplus clay should be cleaned off from the mould using a wooden or plastic spatula, the sprig removed gently from the mould and applied to the pot with slip. Should the clay sprigs tend to stick to the moulds coat the plaster with a little soapy liquid or fine oil before use. Perhaps the best example of sprigging in modern times is to be seen on Wedgewood pottery.

(f) *Stamped ornamentation* — this has been mentioned under the texturing paragraph when objects such as buttons, coins, keys, shells, etc are pressed into the surface of a pot whilst it is still fairly damp. It is also useful to make small stamps of various shapes and designs and biscuit fire them, like the signet stamp used to stamp one's own pottery for easy identification.

(g) *Glass* — coloured glasses mixed together, or even on their own, can give beautiful effects in the bottoms of pots and dishes. Collect different coloured glasses and store in screw top jars after crushing. The pieces of glass should just cover the bottom of the dish after it has been glazed and then placed in the kiln for firing. The results can be quite fascinating. However, it is important that the dish rests absolutely *horizontal* otherwise when the glass melts it will run to one side and harden in that position. Mixing two colours can be very effective, eg blue and green or green and brown. Blend the colours with the glaze that has been chosen to coat the pot.

(h) *Burnishing* — burnishing is probably the simplest form of decoration and is particularly effective with red clay. It is best done when the pot is just beyond the leather-hard stage. Select fairly strong pottery for this purpose and then gently rub the surface in a circular motion with the back of a spoon, a piece of smooth bone or even a stone. A polish will result which will remain after the biscuit firing. This technique is particularly effective on pottery that is to be fired in sawdust or clamp kilns — see Chapter 3.

47

Glazes and decoration

(a) *Underglaze colours* – as already mentioned in Chapter 5, I consider it is best to apply these colours before biscuit firing – this method is specially recommended for use by schools. It is important to realize, however, that it is inadvisable to paint large areas with these colours – outlines or small areas only should be picked out or painted with underglaze colours. If an all over colour is required this is best achieved by using coloured slips at the greenware stage or coloured glazes after biscuit firing.

(b) *Inglaze colouring* – this is the technique of applying colours on top of the unfired glaze. Underglaze colours are used for this and the method of application has already been described in greater detail in Chapter 7. Majolica ware, Faience and Delft are all examples of this type of decoration.

(c) *Wax resist* – the technique for using wax as a resist can be used with glaze decoration in exactly the same way as it is used with slips. It is also possible to mask parts of the pot so that these parts do not absorb the glaze. Some potters even apply wax to the bases of their pots so that they will be free of glaze during firing.

(d) *On-glaze decoration* – this is effected by painting onto the fired glazed pottery on-glaze colours or enamels. These colours need to be mixed with a special oil medium which is obtainable, together with the colours, from pottery suppliers. Brushes and surplus paint can be cleaned by using turpentine or turps substitute. These colours, when applied to the pottery, are then fired to a temperature around 760°C.

Tools

Special mention should be made of the tools used for decoration – particularly brushes. The type of brush used can be very crucial to the end product, for every brush will give a different stroke. It is important, therefore, to take great care of these brushes and to see they are kept clean and supple. Signwriters' brushes and oriental brushes are probably the best, but they are expensive! Select brushes that will give a variety of strokes and use the brushes with a firm movement from the arm, keeping the wrist fairly rigid. Always ensure that tools are washed thoroughly after use so that colours do not get intermixed unintentionally. Remember that it is difficult to remove colours, once applied, and a pot can easily be spoiled with too much haste!

Clay training shoe showing texture of sole and using oxide colouring

48

Decorative uses of glazes

As mentioned in the chapter on glazes, there are many ways of applying glazes to produce different effects and I give below a few examples that are worth mixing and experimenting with:

(a) Transparent green glaze:
2 tsp copper carbonate mixed with hot water (or 1 tsp black copper oxide)
½ litre transparent glaze
Sieve 120 mesh.

(b) Transparent blue glaze:
2 tsp blue stain mixed with hot water (or ½ tsp cobalt oxide)
½ litre transparent glaze
Sieve 120 mesh

(c) Turquoise opaque glaze (pearly):
1-2 tsp black copper oxide mixed with hot water (or 4 tsp copper carbonate)
½ litre white opaque glaze
Sieve 120 mesh

(d) Sky blue opaque glaze:
1 tsp cobalt oxide mixed with hot water (or 4 tsp blue stain)
½ litre white opaque glaze
Sieve 120 mesh

NB If iron oxides are mixed with transparent glazes, shades of browns and yellows are obtained. Pale colours are obtained over grey or buff clays and deep chestnut colours over red clays.

Suggestions

1 Using the above coloured transparent glazes trickle or spray small quantities over pots glazed with white opaque glaze. Domestic plastic spray bottles are quite useful for this purpose. Green transparent glaze over white is very effective as is blue over part green, over white.

2 Take a coloured opaque base glaze and spray over it coloured transparent glazes or pour streaks down the sides of a glazed pot.

3 A pot or tile with depressions in it may be glazed with a coloured opaque glaze, scraped clean over the raised surfaces, leaving a thick deposit of glaze in the indentations. These indentations may be thickened with a brush full of glaze and if fired around $1080°C-1100°C$ a pretty jewel effect will be obtained.

4 Red clay is very suitable for glazing with a white opaque glaze and then further decorating with coloured transparent glazes. The coloured glazes may also be trailed onto the base glaze using a slip trailer or polythene shampoo type bottle with a fine nozzle.

There are many more possibilities so do experiment.

Stoneware glazes

(a) Blue/grey and tenmoku glazes — glaze an incised pot or one with applied decoration with blue/grey glaze, then scrape off the raised surfaces and paint them with tenmoku glaze. The effect will be a superb turquoise and rich brown combination. Coiled pots with the outside of the coils left unsmoothed are very effective when decorated in this manner. A lighter brown effect that be created if the raised surfaces are scraped and left unglazed.

(b) Copper carbonate used with a white stoneware glaze — paint a mixture of copper carbonate and water onto rims or use as a wash on the side of a pot

Detailed texture of a squirrel's
tail compared with the
smoother texture of the owl –
both thumb pots

Right Unglazed terra cotta
head - note use of texture

(eg a slab pot) before biscuit firing. Then glaze with a white stoneware glaze. This technique is very effective on shell and rock sculptures and works very well if hollows are shaded with varying intensities of copper carbonate. Broken glass pieces placed into hollows will give an attractive 'water' effect.

(c) Random pouring of a second glaze – this technique is particularly effective on clay sculptures and large pots. For example, after coating in a white glaze, pour a coloured glaze (slightly thinned with water) over the pot at random, causing a trickled effect. Blue/grey glaze and tenmoku work well when used in this manner and sometimes a good effect is obtained by inverting a pot, either by holding it upside down or by placing it over a bowl on two narrow sticks if it is too heavy to hold easily. Another good combination is iron oxide (red) painted under an oatmeal glaze, eg a grass or fern pattern painted onto the side of a mug before or after glazing with oatmeal.

Banding
Glazes and oxides can be applied to pots by using the banding method. To do this place a pot on a banding wheel (turntable) and hold a wide brush, dipped in an oxide or coloured glaze, against the pot and gently spin the banding wheel. Try not to double coat – single strokes give best results – and don't go round and round with the brush.

Advice
Whenever possible it is desirable to have in mind the type of decoration intended before the pot is even commenced. Pupils should always be encouraged to think ahead. Obviously from time to time one may have second thoughts but generally the best pots are created by those students who have thought through the whole process from the initial choice of clay to the final stages of decoration and glazing. With more advanced students it is advisable to encourage them to produce a rough sketch of the pot to be made and a description of the materials they intend using, before they commence work. If this is done it gives the teacher the opportunity to discuss the various techniques involved and possibly avert unnecessary mistakes.

9 Faults

Unfortunately no matter how carefully pottery is planned and made, from time to time, faults are bound to occur which may cause breakages, glaze imperfections and even ruined pots. This can be a heartbreak situation but if it is possible to analyze the cause then a repetition is unlikely to occur. It is when a fault recurs frequently that problems really begin.

In this chapter I intend to take a look at some of the most common faults and consider their causes. Even the occasional fault can be extremely vexing and particularly so if there is no obvious solution.

Repairing breakages

(a) Greenware — should a piece of pottery break before it has been fired it may be difficult to mend unless the clay is heavily grogged. Grogged clays, such as crank or sculpting marl can usually be rejoined with light sponging and a little slip. However, if a piece of a pot made from a smooth clay breaks off it is much more difficult to mend. In such cases the pot and pieces must be gently sponged over, wrapped in a damp cloth and placed in a sealed airtight polythene bag for a couple of days. When the pieces have returned to a damp condition they can then be joined together again using slip. It is important that the pot be allowed to dry slowly. If speed is essential dry pieces of unfired clay can sometimes be joined successfully by using vinegar, instead of water or slip, lightly brushed over the broken edges. The vinegar reacts with the surface clay causing it to form a sticky slip which will aid the joining of the broken pieces. It is an interesting chemical process and the technique is worth experimenting with.

(b) Biscuitware — when biscuit-fired pottery breaks it is usually not worth keeping unless it is possible to glaze the pieces separately and join them, after firing, with a strong glue. Occasionally it is possible to balance the glazed piece or pieces on the glazed pot and fire it. Then, it is hoped, the glaze will fuse the pieces together and act as 'glue'. Unfortunately these methods usually leave a hairline so are not always satisfactory.

Causes of breakages and imperfections during biscuit firing

(a) Breakages —if a pot breaks or blows up in the biscuit-fired kiln it is often due to the fact that the pot or parts of the pot have been made solid or too thick. Walls of uneven thickness may also cause problems due to uneven shrinkage during firing. Another common cause of a pot blowing up is when it has been packed into the biscuit kiln before it is *really* dry. Handles and added parts to pots will often fall off a pot during firing if they were not in the same damp state when joined. Remember that a pot that varies considerably in its thickness or one which has dried too rapidly will cause uneven contractions of the clay and will invariably crack or break during biscuit firing. One possible way of solving the problem of firing these pots is to ensure that

51

Overfired kiln showing damage to kiln and to pottery inside – note it has melted into a solid mass

they are absolutely dry and that the temperature of the biscuit kiln is raised very, very slowly.

(b) Mending cracks – cracks that appear in the biscuit firing of the pot are usually caused by poor joining of seams in the initial making. They can be filled with a special filler or 'stopping' that can be purchased from pottery suppliers. To do this wet the crack to be filled and fill with a stiff mixture of stopping (usually mixed with water). Then refire the pot to biscuit temperature before glazing. Household fire cement, can also be used quite satisfactorily for this purpose.

(c) Air bubbles – if the biscuit fired pottery has bulges in it, this is usually due to trapped air in the clay before firing and is caused by insufficient wedging and kneading or, possibly, failure to prick out air bubbles in the plastic clay mass, when making the pot.

(d) Plaster of paris – small grains of plaster may contaminate the plastic clay and cause many problems at later stages. In the biscuit-fired-ware, pieces of pottery will blow or crack off leaving a hole or broken face edge – it is usually possible to see the speck of plaster at the base of the hole. Occasionally a small speck of plaster will survive the biscuit fired stage but will cause part of the glaze-fired pot to erupt – maybe several weeks after it has been removed from the kiln! The only remedy is to ensure that plaster of paris never comes into contact with plastic clay – *always* throw away any clay that has become contaminated or keep it well apart in a clearly labelled bin, to be used only for mould making. Of course, it is best not to use plaster of paris at all in a clay area, then unfortunate accidents cannot occur.

Underglaze colours and oxides

Blistering: this is usually caused by the colours being applied too thickly. Sometimes the effect will be to create a black metallic surface that is devoid of colour and will not absorb glaze.

Problems with glaze firing

These can be many and varied but a few of the most common are:

(a) Crazing or cracking – usually due to the fact that the glaze has been applied too thickly or the pottery has been cooled too quickly after firing, often caused by the kiln door being opened too soon. A mismatched glaze can occasionally cause this problem, ie the glaze does not match the clay body used and the glaze may shrink more rapidly than the clay, – the simple answer is to buy clays and glazes from the same supplier; fortunately this problem does not often occur with educational materials.

(b) Crawling – this is when the glaze crawls away in patches from some areas of the pot, leaving them bare. The cause is often dust or grease on the pot and, sometimes, too thick a layer of glaze being applied to the pot. This fault can sometimes be remedied by heating the pot to around 200°C, reglazing the bare patches and refiring. I do not find this a very satisfactory solution – take better care next time!

(c) Blistering – usually due to a bad glaze or one which has the wrong balance of ingredients. If the glaze used is a 'home-made' glaze, check the weight ratio next time.

(d) Runny and bubbling glaze – if the glaze runs down the pot or has a

52

rather unpleasant molten look about it, the cause is usually over-firing. Sometimes the cause can be in the glaze itself and then the addition of a little china clay or flint may help. Occasionally this bubbling effect can be due to underfiring when the surface of the pot is still dry.

(e) Peeling or flaking — this is the opposite of crawling and is due to the body shrinking more than the glaze.

(f) Starved glaze — this is caused by the glaze being too thin when applied to the pot. It may be that there is too much water mixed in with the glaze or quite simply that the glaze in the bucket is not kept stirred — hence more water than glaze is applied.

(g) Stuck ware — when pots in a glaze-fired kiln have been allowed to touch they will invariably stick together and the only remedy is to attempt to break them apart and then to file or grind the sharp edges where they have been joined. In the case of stuck shelves, when pottery has stuck to the shelves due to a runny glaze the only solution is to try soaking shelf and pottery in hot water for an hour or so — they will generally part company fairly easily and only a little cleaning up (grinding or filing) will be necessary. To prevent this happening again ensure the shelves are coated with bat wash and silica sand and check the quality of the glazes used. Also check the firing temperatures used for respective glazes.

(h) Colours firing away — this is usually due to over-firing which causes the colours to decompose but, of course, it can be due to colours being applied *too* thinly.

(i) Bloated pottery — this occurs when a pot is overfired at the glaze-firing stage causing the clay body not only to vitrify but to begin to melt, causing bubbles to form.

(j) Warped pottery — this is due to unevenness in the making and walls of the pottery, or to over-firing.

(k) Powdery glass — when using pieces of broken glass to decorate pottery at the glazing stage, it is advisable to fire to as high a temperature as possible. Sometimes a white film or blobs of a soda type substance tend to form on the surface of the glass when it has been fired to only earthenware temperatures, even though the glass has melted properly. This white powder can be wiped off with a damp cloth and will disappear completely after a few weeks. However, glass fired to stoneware temperatures will not have this problem.

(l) Adjustment of glaze consistencies — should a biscuit fired pot be over fired, causing problems with the glaze adhering and being absorbed by the pot, reheat the pot before attempting to glaze it and whilst it is still hot glaze it with a slightly thicker glaze. Conversely, if the pot is underfired, do *not* heat the pot but thin the glaze by adding more water as in this state the pottery will be more absorbent than usual.

(m) Filling cracks in white glazed pottery — A mixture of strong glue (one with a fixer) and zinc oxide makes a very satisfactory filler and requires no further firing.

10 Pottery wheels

To the uninitiated the word 'pottery' and using a potter's wheel are synonymous and some people even think that a pot which has not been made on a wheel is not really pottery. This, of course, is not true, for all pots made from clay and fired in a kiln are indeed 'pottery'. However, when you teach pottery one of the first questions you will be asked is 'When can I use the wheel?' The potter's wheel has a strange fascination for most people and those who master it are easily hypnotised by its magic.

Choosing a wheel

Before one can become involved in the fascinating process of throwing clay, a wheel must be obtained and this can be quite an expensive business. There are many different types of potters' wheels on the market today, varying in cost from a hundred pounds to over four hundred pounds, if you buy new. Secondhand wheels are worth looking out for but seem to be very scare. An ordinary standard kick wheel is about the cheapest, then about fifty pounds dearer is a geared kick wheel which leads into the range of electrically powered wheels costing between two and four hundred pounds. Provided you are not aiming to make really large pots, such as cider jars, and are content with normal domestic ware a portable bench wheel, which will take up to 2½ kg of clay, is probably the most suitable choice. The Wengers Portable Bench Wheel (model 2805W) is the wheel I would recommend for most schools as its height is dependent on the height of the bench it is placed on and so can be adapted for use by young children and grown men alike. It is easily cleaned and can be moved from place to place with minimum effort, if so required. The larger and more expensive wheels are ideal for use by those who have the experience or wish to learn to throw much larger pots. Some of these have seats attached to them but all are made for adult use and young or small people usually experience physical problems. In the end, though, the choice usually comes down to personal preference and available finance.

The next question that is frequently posed is how old should a child be before he can be expected to use a potter's wheel satisfactorily? The answer to this question is not simple as it depends very much on the child's co-ordination and control of his hands. Most top juniors can manage to use a wheel quite well and do produce some very acceptable little pots. If possible it is worth allowing children to start using a wheel at around nine years of age — that is, of course, provided the wheel is set at a suitable height. A useful guide as to the best height is that they should be able to lean over the wheel so that their noses are directly above the centre of the wheelhead.

When teaching the use of a potter's wheel one is often quite surprised by those who prove to be the most talented. Frequently the child (or adult) who is least talented in other directions will prove to have a special affinity and ability for working with the wheel. Of course, it is very important that the foundations are laid by thorough initial teaching of the processes.

In this chapter I list the points that I find particularly helpful in the

teaching of throwing and turning on a potter's wheel. I do not delve into the finer details of the art as many superb books have already been written on the subject with photographs illustrating each step. In my opinion, the best book available today is John Colbeck's book, *Pottery, the Technique of Throwing* and I recommend it to any teacher to keep as a 'Bible' on the subject. A useful tip for using this book is to select a page, place the opened book in a polythene bag and sit it up in front of the wheel for reference. The stages are extremely easy to follow, and the polythene will prevent the book being damaged by splashing clay.

Left Note position of body whilst throwing a pot on a potter's wheel

Thinning the rim of a pot. Note position of arms and hands — they are controlled and rest on the bowl rim providing a levering action

Using a potter's wheel

Basically the technique of using a potter's wheel can be divided into two processes — throwing and turning. A pot may be thrown without the follow up of being turned but a pot cannot be turned unless it has first been thrown! (There is one exception to this last statement when, occasionally, a potter may turn a hand-built pot for decorative purposes.)

Throwing: this is the process of shaping an even mass of soft plastic clay, using one's hands on a revolving wheelhead at varying speeds which are controlled by the thrower.

Turning: this is a process whereby a potter pares away excess clay from a leather-hard form, using sharp tools and whilst the wheelhead is rotating slowly. The leather-hard form is usually slightly reshaped during this process.

Throwing and turning are often thought to be difficult to learn but this is not so, provided basic rules are followed and in the correct order. As in all motor-

55

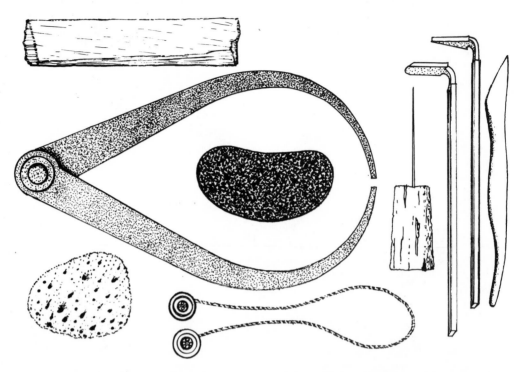

Tools for use with a potter's wheel

activities regular practice is essential, but little and often, rather than a long stint at one go, will prove to be much more productive. Provided one sets oneself high standards and is self critical, progress will not be difficult. It may well be compared to the process of learning to ride a bicycle — there are bound to be occasional falls and some hurt more than others!

Before attempting to throw a pot, first select a suitable throwing clay — usually one containing a small percentage of fine grog. Then, when it has been wedged and kneaded sufficiently, make it up into balls. If the intention is to make several similar pots of the same size (eg a set of mugs) it is advisable to weigh the balls of clay accurately. in this way the chances of success will be greatly improved — at least the starting point will be with balls of clay of the same size! I have listed below guidelines for the beginner but it is, of course, always better if the teacher first demonstrates the process, describing what he is doing and why, as the pot is thrown.

Initial guidelines for throwing a pot

1 Wedge and knead clay and ensure it is soft enough to drop a thumb into it gently.

2 Make up balls of clay that can comfortably be encircled by both hands (usually about the size of a cricket ball) and keep to hand under polythene so that they do not dry out.

3 Check your tool-kit and be sure that you have in it all the tools likely to be needed for the throwing process — there is nothing worse than having to stop to find something with messy hands. Basic needs are a bowl of water, a small sponge, a needle, a cutting wire and small boards for placing the pots on to dry. It is also useful to have a scraper, a pointed turning tool and a small piece of balsa wood.

4 Check that there is a container to collect waste water from the wheel

56

tray if it is the type that has a drainage plug and hose.

5 Ensure the turntable is *dry* and clean. (A piece of balsa wood scraped across the surface of the turntable will remove any damp clay and dry it at the same time.)

6 Place a ball of clay firmly onto the centre of the turntable and pat into shape.

7 Wet both hands and sprinkle a little water over the clay.

8 Check your stance — this is *very* important. Lean down over the wheel with your full weight being taken by your forearms which should rest on the rim of the wheel-tray. Your nose should be directly above the centre of the turntable and the clay ball. By maintaining this stance you should not lose control and it should be easy to use your hands in a levering action.

9 Switch wheel on to *full* speed and with hands firmly around the clay draw it up into a cone shape and then down again into a ball shape — repeat this action several times. This technique will assist with the centring of the clay and also 'condition' it.

10 Keep the clay and hands wet from now on for if the clay dries it will stick to your hands and pull the pot off the wheel.

11 When the clay is centred, with back edges of hands resting on the revolving turntable drop right thumb into the centre of the clay and draw outwards, steadying the clay with the left palm. Smooth the base (inside) of the pot at this stage.

12 Slow speed of wheel down to around half of the original speed.

13 The actual throwing process — resting forearms on the rim of the tray and keeping both hands touching, lift the side of the opened clay form gently upwards in a levering motion. When your fingers reach the rim of the pot, remove them *gently* and *slowly*. Often the knuckle of the right forefinger is used in this process — hence the term *knuckling*.

14 Repeat this action several times, ensuring that the lifting movements are at roughly the same speed as that at which the turntable is rotating.

15 During this throwing process the pot should be shaped by exerting gentle pressure from the inside or onto the outside of the pot.

16 It is important to remember that as you are constantly wetting the surface of the clay so the excess water from the inside of the pot must be removed, using the sponge. If it is a tall pot, use a dottle (a sponge tied to the end of a stick). Do not allow your hands to dry but keep them, the pot and wheelhead as clean as possible whilst throwing — mess confuses.

17 Should the rim become uneven (this is usually due to the clay moving out of centre at some stage) then hold a pin firmly to the edge as the pot revolves and the uneven piece of clay can easily be removed. It may be necessary, at this stage, to clean the base and bevel it with a scraper.

18 For final smoothing, hold the sponge or turning tool gently against the pot whilst it revolves.

19 To remove the pot — stop the wheel, splash the turntable with water and pull the wire or fishing line gently between the pot and turntable. With *dry* fingers move the pot gently to the edge of the turntable by its base, slide it off the turntable onto the palm of your hand and gently place onto a board to dry. Do *not* try to slide the pot directly from the turntable onto a board — many a catastrophe has occurred in this way. A little practice will make perfect!

20 Pots should be allowed to dry slowly and when 'leather hard' should be inverted, allowing the base to dry or, alternatively, the pot should be replaced centrally on the wheelhead in preparation for a foot to be turned. In order to stick the rim of the pot to the turntable, lightly moisten the rim and the turntable and press down gently causing a seal to form. If this is not satisfactory three or four knobs of soft clay pressed down onto the turntable against the pot will secure the pot whilst it is turned.

Notes and tips for teaching

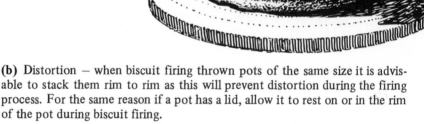

(a) Newspaper — when removing a pot from the wheel with a wide rim it is useful to gently place a sheet of wet newspaper over the rim before cutting it off the turntable. This will prevent the shape of the pot distorting as it is removed and as it dries.

(b) Distortion — when biscuit firing thrown pots of the same size it is advisable to stack them rim to rim as this will prevent distortion during the firing process. For the same reason if a pot has a lid, allow it to rest on or in the rim of the pot during biscuit firing.

(c) Safety — before allowing pupils to use a pottery wheel do check that they do not have long hair loose — tie it back and be safe.

(d) Aprons — complaints from parents will be avoided if good covering aprons or overalls are used by pupils — the beginner using the wheel usually gets smothered with wet clay!

(e) Nails — long finger nails are a nuisance as they score the clay and damage pots. They can also be very painful if they get torn.

(f) Balsa wood — keep odd pieces of balsa wood as they are the best aid that I have found for cleaning and drying the wheelhead.

(g) Hands — always remove hands from a revolving pot *slowly* — a slight nudge can ruin it.

(h) Air bubbles — if an air bubble should appear in the wall of a pot that is being thrown, prick it open with the needle and gently add soft clay to the hole. Carry on with the throwing process.

(i) Speeds — it is important to remember that the wheelhead must rotate quickly when centring the clay and then be reduced to a low speed for the actual making of the pot.

Variations using the wheel

(a) *Agate ware:* this is a very attractive form of pottery and is made by colouring several different pieces of clay (using stains or oxides as explained

58

in Chapter 8) and twisting them together in a spiral action. The mixed clays are lightly kneaded together and a pot is thrown on the wheel. When leather hard the pot will require to be scraped or turned for the various coloured clays to show their agate type patterns. After biscuit firing this form of pottery only requires to be decorated with a transparent glaze.

(b) *Thrown necks:* a very effective technique is to throw just a neck (a cone with no base to it) and add it to a wrap pot. This will produce an elegant bottle if the proportions are considered and a suitable decoration is used.

(c) *Tiles:* attractive tiles can be made by throwing small shapes and rings and then applying them with slip to damp clay tiles. This technique can be particularly effective if coloured clays are used or even a grey clay on a red tile background.

(d) *Handles:* if handles are to be added to pots they must always be pulled in the correct manner and *not* formed by rolling out a piece of clay and 'sticking it on'. To do this correctly take a plastic sausage sized roll of clay and, keeping it wet, pull the handle downwards. If you hold the clay over a bowl of water you can dip your hand into it on the down stroke of each pulling action. Always ensure that when joining a handle to a pot that both are at the same damp state, ie nearly leather hard. Score the surfaces to be joined and paint pot and handle with slip before pressing into position. John Colbeck gives an excellent description of this process in his revised edition of *The Technique of Pottery* by Dora Billington.

(e) *Used clay:* do not throw clay which has been used on the wheel into the recycling bin. It may be too soft for immediate re-use but put it aside to harden a little and then re-knead it ready for use. Putting it into the bin with other forms of recycled clay will mix it with clay of different consistencies and so make it much more difficult to prepare for throwing again. Keep your throwing clay in a separate bin and, if it gets 'tired', allow it to rest for a week or so. Then add a little new clay and re-knead it — it will be as good as new and ready for use again.

(f) *Identification:* remember to put a mark of identification on your thrown pots. It is particularly effective and 'professional' to have one's own stamp handy to impress at the base of handles on mugs and jugs. Certainly, teachers must see that their pupils do this or at a later stage recognition of individual pots can be very difficult.

Maintenance of pottery wheels

Pottery wheels do not need a lot of maintenance but it is advisable to have them serviced by a qualified engineer about once a year. They should not be placed too near to radiators, particularly if they have grease nipples as these will tend to dry out quickly. Keep a grease gun handy and give them a 'shot' once or twice a term. It is also necessary to check the bearings and grease them if necessary.

If wheels are cleaned and well washed after use (every time!) they should not get clogged up and few problems are likely to occur. Remember the tip given earlier (Chapter 2) when I suggested all switches — and that includes press button switches — should be covered with polythene. The polythene, if supple, does not impede the action of the switch but prevents it becoming clogged up by clay impregnated fingers. Lastly, check regularly that electric cables are in good condition and do not trail around to be tripped over — tie them to the wall or to the wheel if they are excessively long.

11 Exhibiting pottery

There seems to be very little advice available regarding the ways and means of exhibiting pottery to advantage. Over the years I have read many pottery books but found in them very little reference to this subject. The questions that usually need to be answered are: How best to select items of pottery? and How best to exhibit them? Generally the decisions have to be made by those setting up and co-ordinating an exhibition and so personal preference may often prevail. Selection can be very difficult for tastes differ considerably.

Most people, and children in particular, are very vain about their pottery and love others to look at it and comment on it. For this reason, an exhibition of a group's work can be a very exciting occasion and the work building up to it usually produces a very high standard with a variety of problems being solved *en route*. It is amazing how much more is learned when there is concentrated work, due to a deadline date being set. I think that perhaps the best example of this type of 'spurt' is shown during the last six weeks before an 'O' level or an 'A' level examination — and an exhibition seems to produce a similar effect.

For many years I have been responsible for the setting up and general co-ordination of a large pottery exhibition held each year in the exhibition area and the children's section of our local library. Contributors to this exhibition are children and teachers of all ages — from five to 65 from 30 to 40 schools in the district. The enthusiasm for these exhibitions has always been most rewarding and the public interest is enormous. The exhibition usually lasts for a month and always there are people looking and commenting. Perhaps the most disappointing aspect for the general public is that, having had their interest in pottery whetted, they then find that there are not enough evening

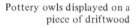
Pottery owls displayed on a piece of driftwood

Tiles and figures grouped to form a complete picture

and part-time classes available. It is, therefore, the school children, in this day and age, who have the greatest advantage and it is pleasing to see that they make such good use of the opportunities offered to them. The standard of work is, in most cases, excellent and it is most pleasing to see how it improves year after year.

We are fortunate that our local press is interested and supports these exhibitions. It always produces a good article and photographs, so that the public are aware of what is going on. This, I feel, is a most important factor — there is little point in spending hours and hours organizing such an exhibition and encouraging people to make for it if there is no recognition, and it is very saddening to hear someone say at a later date 'if only I had known'. Parents and relations of children and the children themselves are very proud when their own particular piece of pottery is put on show, so once an exhibition is held the excitement continues to build up from year to year. One of the outstanding advantages of an exhibition of pottery, or any craft, is that new ideas are stimulated and often seeds are sown for years to come. For this reason colour slides of various aspects of the work shown are a great asset and can be particularly useful if duplicate sets can be kept at a teachers' centre enabling schools to borrow them for class discussion.

Organization, selection and display

Here are some ideas for ways of organizing an exhibition of pottery, whether it be large or small.

(a) *Title* — I have found that it's very helpful to suggest a broadly outlined title for an exhibition. This needs to be suggested about four to five months prior to the handing-in date to enable those who wish to make pottery especially for it, to do so. The ideal choice of title is something topical — such as 'The Silver Jubilee', 'The Year of the Child' or 'All Creatures Great and Small'. The title should not govern the sole theme of the exhibition but should be used as a guide for those requiring one. Primary schools particularly enjoy working around a theme as they can often integrate it with other subjects on the curriculum. Senior schools tend to use a theme less as, by this time, they are often specializing. Very often work will be submitted for

61

exhibition that has no relationship at all to the title but this should be quite acceptable provided there is quality. Variety is always an exhibition asset and is bound to occur with the more senior students who are really beginning to develop their own style.

(b) *Selection and display* — I always find it best to group pottery displays according to age range as far as is possible. For example I put infant and junior school work in the children's section of the library and the middle school, senior school and teachers' work in the adjacent main exhibition area. The next problem is usually the setting and what to display the pottery on. I have been very fortunate in this area to be able to borrow tables from the School Meals Services, who have always been most helpful in this respect. I use these tables in the display area for there are already very nicely carpeted boxes of different heights in the children's library which are ideal for displaying small pieces of pottery if used in conjunction with a few drapes.

If mounting an exhibition of any size, away from home territory, it is advisable to ask those submitting pottery to label each item on the underside of the pot. Do not place name cards in front of the pots as the cards usually succeed in hiding the best! It is also a good idea to number the pots and keep a check list of pot number, owner and school. If recognition of individual pieces of pottery is desired the best way to achieve this is to stick a small number on each piece and to relate the numbers on a list to the names of the owners. The list can then be pinned up for all to see or placed on the table alongside the pottery. The most important and, indeed, the most difficult thing regarding display is the tendency to overcrowd the pottery. Usually there is too much pottery for the area available and so invariably, rather than offend, it all has to be put out. However, do bear in mind that, whenever possible, it is best to place larger pieces in a setting where there is space around. Don't make the area look too busy.

It is a great advantage to the final display arrangement if pottery can be shown on different levels and for this it is wise to collect different sized boxes and blocks of polystyrene. Cover these with carefully selected plain (if possible) coloured drapes or old curtains, allowing the material to fall in folds where suitable and place the pots strategically around. It is also important to consider the light factor, whether it be natural or artificial, and to study the backgrounds. If display boards are available it is often an added attraction to pin up a few working sketches that relate to the pottery being shown. Tiles, tile pictures and pottery collage look very well on these boards. The grouping of pieces of pottery is very important and they should, if possible, relate in some way – be it type of decoration, subject matter or size. Background colour must be looked at very critically for if it does not contrast well the pottery will be lost.

(c) Judging – this is a debatable point but something I do not favour, particularly with pottery. Everyone who has offered a piece of pottery for display has done their individual best and I do not consider it fair to try and judge one piece to be better than another. It is fair to say that technical ability can be judged fairly but from then on it must often be personal preference and I believe that this kind of selection only causes grievances that need not arise – let it *all* be admired! Who are we to say what is best? I think that test should be left to the examiners when such judgements *have* to be made. I have noticed that competition often tends to create inhibition, which is most unfortunate.

(d) Taking down an exhibition – is a sad time but provided the pieces exhibited have been named with a school code (if away from home) and their respective packing boxes also named, nothing should go astray or be broken – especially if each piece is individually wrapped in newspaper before it is put into the box. Encourage teachers to unpack, display and repack their own pottery wherever possible. This sense of involvement is usually greatly appreciated as the context of the individual displays is not lost as can sometimes happen when a 'stranger' sets up work. In this way most people seem to end up happy with the results and the load is spread.

Do exhibit pottery whenever possible. A pottery exhibition gives so much pleasure to so many people and really is worth all the effort but do so before all those peices of pottery disappear home to be given to grandma or to sit on the mantlepiece – they are very hard to get back again when you want them.

In this chapter I have talked mainly about the larger exhibitions incorporating the work of several schools or groups. However, equally important, is the small display of pots that is so often seen in the entrance hall of a school – or even in the classroom – and basically the same rules apply however large or small the display or exhibition may be. Arrange the pieces carefully, consider contrasting colours between pots and background and group pottery simply so as not to make it appear too busy. Allow space wherever possible as a jumble of pots causes visual confusion. The most important thing is to allow the work to be seen!

Pottery head mounted on a wooden plinth

Making pottery pay

Pottery can easily pay for itself and it is, therefore, a good idea to charge a small sum of money for the pieces of pottery that are to be taken home. Not only will the pots be appreciated more, but in this way a small fund can be created to provide more glazes or colours which will enhance future projects. A good method of establishing a price other than by feel or intuition, is by weighing and charging, eg a penny per ounce – but do keep a cash record. A school fair or sale of work naturally provides a wonderful shop window for any stray pieces of pottery that are unclaimed, or for those pieces that have been made specially for the occasion. It is a good idea at these times to persuade pupils to make one pot for themselves and one for the sale! Remember, of course, that the pottery displayed for sale is also a form of exhibition – if displayed well it will have a higher value.

63

Stoneware slab pot – note contrasting texture

12 Techniques and ideas

Although it has not been my intention in this book to elaborate on techniques for making different types of pottery, it occurs to me that a list of ideas for things that can be made from various techniques could be helpful to teachers.

Clay — thumbed and pinched

Animals, cartoon characters, imitation stones and rocks, pomanders, ocarinas, bowls and delicate shell shapes.

Clay — rolled out flat

(a) Wrap pots: vases, tree pots, logs, mugs, totem poles and castles.
(b) Leaf dishes: single and multiple dishes and plates, also leaf vases and leaf decoration.
(c) Jewellery: pendants, cuff-links, necklaces, ear-rings.
(d) Masks: Haloween and Guy Fawkes made over paper humps.
(e) Figures: wrapped around a cardboard cone — Nativity, etc.
(f) Tiles: free form and using a tile cutter — collage, book ends, slab pots, tile pictures, night-lights.
(g) Press moulded dishes: dishes and bottles with coiled necks.
(h) Slab pots: shallow dishes and tall pots, boxes, chests of drawers, sculptures.
(i) Flags: incised patterns or built up with coils.
(j) Bag pots: all shapes and sizes made by wrapping clay around a bag filled with sand which is poured out at the leather hard stage.

Pinch pots and thumb pots

64

Hollow models — lady and gentleman (stoneware)

Thumbed and squeezed animals (earthenware)

Clay — coiled

(a) Brick pots: (using red and grey clays) houses, wishing wells, farm buildings, villages, forts.
(b) Animals: two coils joined at the middle and a thumb pot head.
(c) Coil pots: vases, lamp bases, jugs, sculptures, coiled necks for bottles, flower-pot holders, pots for macrame use.

Clay — thrown

Mugs, jugs, vases, casseroles, dishes, bowls, plates, sculptures.

Roller skate and snail – biscuit
fired and painted

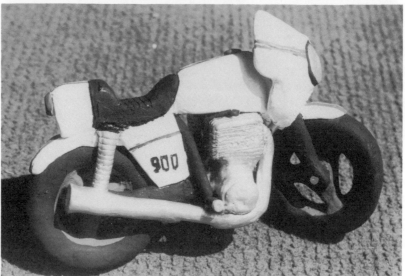

Motor cycle – biscuit fired
and painted

Veteran car – stoneware glazed

66

GLOSSARY

Agate: Pottery made from entwining coloured clays.

Ash glaze: A glaze made from a wood ash and a clay, such as china clay. Different ashes create different colours and textures to glazes.

Ball clay: A plastic secondary clay which will fire to a high temperature.

Banding wheel: An unpowered turntable which can be used on a table for painting horizontal bands on to pottery or for supporting hand-built pots whilst being made.

Bat: A kiln shelf made from fireclay or a wooden board for working on.

Bentonite: An ingredient added to glazes and slips as a suspender.

Biscuit: Unglazed pottery that has been fired once — usually to around 960°C for educational purposes.

Bloating: Blisters in the body of the pot usually occurring during glaze firing and caused by pressure exerted by gases which are trapped within the partially fused body.

Body: This is another word for the clay used to make pottery.

Burnishing: The technique of polishing leather-hard clay by rubbing it with the back of a spoon or a smooth stone.

Casting: To make pottery shapes by pouring liquid clay (slip) into a porous plaster of paris mould.

Cone: A triangular shaped cone which has a known melting point and is placed inside a kiln to indicate the temperature reached at a given stage.

Crank: Refractory support for tiles, plates, etc.

Crawling: When the fired glaze shrinks away from the body leaving bare patches. Often caused by dust or grease on the pottery before glazing.

Crazing: The appearance of fine cracking lines in the glaze caused by excessive contraction of the glaze during cooling. The pot then usually becomes porous as the glaze 'seal' is broken.

Cutting off: Pulling a thin wire or fishing line between pot and wheelhead before sliding it off.

Deflocculant: The addition of an electrolyte such as sodium silicate and soda ash causes the clay slip or glaze to disperse and become more fluid.

Dottle: A sponge on the end of a stick used for cleaning and smoothing the inside of tall pots.

Dunting: When cold air gets into a kiln whilst it is cooling, causing the pots to crack or break.

Earthenware: A fairly porous pottery made from clay which is fired to a temperature below that at which it would vitrify — usually around 1060°C–1080°C for educational purposes.

Enamels: Low temperature coloured glazes — usually brightly coloured — that are applied, mostly by brush, onto a pre-fired high temperature glaze.

Feathering: A technique of decoration using a feather or a bristle and gently dragging it across lines of wet coloured slip.

Fettling: The removal of seams and marks caused usually by casting moulds. The leather-hard clay is scraped with a knife or metal kidney and/or sponged.

Firing: The heating up of a kiln packed with pottery to a temperature that will make the clay and/or the glaze hard and permanent.

Fuse: To heat to melting point.

Glaze: A thin layer of glass covering a biscuit fired pot. Usually the biscuit fired pot is dipped, brushed or sprayed with a suspension of ground glaze in water and then fired to high temperature.

Glost: The actual firing of glazed ware in a kiln.

Greenware: Unfired clayware.

Grog: A sand-like material made from ground-up biscuit ware which is added to clay to give it strength and reduce shrinkage.

Handbuilding: The term used for building pottery or making pots in any way other than by using a potter's wheel or mechanical means. It usually refers to methods such as slab building, coiling or pinching.

Incising: A form of decoration — marking and incising the surface of leather-hard clay with tools.

Kidney: A kidney shaped flat rubber or metal tool, useful for smoothing and finishing handbuilt pottery and pots made on a wheel.

Kiln: An oven for firing pottery to a very high temperature. A kiln can be fuelled by electricity, gas, oil or solid fuels.

Kiln furniture: A term used to describe the refractory pieces used in a kiln to support and separate the shelves and pieces of pottery during firing.

Knuckling up: The action of raising a pot on a wheel by gently squeezing the wall of the pot between the knuckle of the first finger of the right hand and the middle finger of the left hand.

Lawn: A fine mesh sieve supported by a frame and used in pottery for passing liquid slips and glazes through.

Leather-hard: A term used for clay that has partly dried to a stage when it can be cut like leather, using a knife. At this stage the clay is still damp enough to join handles, knobs, etc, with slip, to a pot in the same condition. It is the ideal state for turning, fettling and sponging. Another name for this stage is cheese-hard.

Maturing temperature: This is the term to describe the temperature reached when a glaze will have properly fused or when clay has been fired to its correct strength.

Opening up: Inserting the thumb of the right hand into the centred ball of clay and drawing it outwards.

Once fired: A term used when pottery is made, glazed and fired in one operation — sometimes called 'clay glazing' or raw glazing.

On-glaze: A form of decoration whereby metal oxides and stains are applied on top of the unfired glaze.

Over-firing: When pottery has reached a temperature in the kiln in excess of its optimum temperature. The pottery is often distorted and, if glazed, the pots frequently stick to the kiln shelves.

Oxides: Metal-based clay or glaze colourants.

Pinholing: Usually a fault in the glaze or clay body, causing tiny bubbles of trapped air to break through the glaze or body at high temperature.

Plasticity: The quality that clay has when it can be shaped easily and yet retain its new shape.

Porcelain: White translucent stoneware clay, firing to temperatures in excess of 1300°C.

Porous: The porous state of biscuit ware will indicate the thickness of the glaze to be used. It relates to the amount of pore space in the ware.

Primary: A primary clay is a pure clay.

Props: Supports that separate kiln shelves.

Pugging: (pug mill) The action of reconstituting clay by passing it through a pug mill, which is a form of mincing machine.

Pulling: Pulling handles is the action of stroking plastic clay downwards with water, using the hands.

Pyrometer: A clock-type temperature indicator sited near to a kiln and attached to a thermocouple which is inserted into the kiln in order to record the internal temperature of the kiln.

Raku: A thick type of low fired earthenware, used in Japan for the traditional tea ceremony. The pots are removed from the kiln, whilst it is still firing, with tongs and then plunged into water. Sometimes they are first plunged into leaves or sawdust to produce varying colour effects.

Refractory clays: Those clays capable of withstanding high temperatures, in excess of 1300°C. Stoneware and porcelain clays are examples of these.

Rolling guides: Sticks of wood approximately 356 mm long x 6 mm thick used in conjunction with a rolling pin to produce rolled clay of even thickness.

Secondary clays: These are clays that contain a variety of minerals and are, consequently, not pure.

Sgraffito: A form of decoration whereby an outer coating of clay or glaze is scratched through with a sharp tool to expose the different colour beneath.

Slip: A liquid clay with the consistency of double cream used in conjunction with colouring oxides for decoration. Also used for slip moulding.

Slip trailing: A decorative process for creating designs by forcing liquid clay through a narrow nozzle attached to a bag or bottle. Like icing a cake.

Slurry: An alternative name for slip.

Soak: To hold the temperature of a kiln steady for about 20 minutes. This will improve the quality of certain glazes.

Sponging: Cleaning the surface of clayware prior to firing using a damp sponge.

Sprigging: A form of decoration by fixing small moulded shapes to the surface of a pot of a different colour, eg Wedgwood.

Stains: Colours prepared from oxides for staining clays and glazes.

Stoneware: Pottery fired to a temperature above 1200°C and which is vitreous (non-porous) and opaque.

Texturing: A decorative process applied to clay whilst it is still soft causing a roughened or indented surface.

Throwing: The making of a pot with the hands, a potter's wheel and plastic clay.

Turning: Trimming thrown pots at the leather-hard stage to remove excess clay, using a potter's wheel and sharp metal tools.

Underglaze: Oxides and stains applied to green-ware prior to biscuit firing and then glazed.

Vitrify: To fire to a glassy state which is non-porous.

Wax resist: A wax applied to a biscuit fired pot so that it will resist glaze. Usually applied to parts of a pot as a decorative process.

Weathering: Leaving clay outside exposed to the weather.

Wedging: The de-airing process of clay by hand. The lump of clay is repeatedly cut and thrown down hard on to a solid work bench.

Wheel: A revolving turntable controlled by the potter's feet or by electricity. It can revolve at varying speeds according to the potter's requirements.

RECOMMENDED SUPPLIERS for educational materials and equipment

Acme Marls Limited
(Kiln shelves and furniture)
Clough Street,
Hanley,
Stoke-on-Trent, ST1 4AF

Deancraft Limited
Lovatt Street,
Stoke-on-Trent, ST4 7RL

The Fulham Pottery Ltd,
(General materials)
210, New Kings Road,
London, SW6 4NY
Telephone: 01-731 2167

Harrison Mayer Ltd,
(General materials)
Meir,
Stoke-on-Trent, ST3 7PX
Telephone: (0782) 316111

Hymus Engineering Company,
(Kilns and pugmills)
West Station Goods Yard,
Maldon,
Essex, CM9 6SG
Telephone: (0621) 52391

Podmore Ceramics Ltd,
(General materials)
105, Minet Road,
London, SW9 7UH
Telephone: 01-737 3636

Podmore & Sons Ltd,
(General materials)
Shelton, Stoke-on-Trent,
Staffordshire,
Telephone: (0782) 24571

Potclays Limited,
(Clays)
Albion Works
Brickkiln Lane,
Etruria,
Stoke-on-Trent
Telephone: (0782) 29816

Wengers Ltd,
(General materials)
Etruria,
Stoke-on-Trent, ST4 7BQ
Telephone: (0782) 25126

BIBLIOGRAPHY

Dora M Billington, revised by John Colbeck *The Technique of Pottery* Batsford

John Colbeck *Pottery, the Technique of Throwing* Batsford

Michael Casson *The Craft of the Potter* BBC

Bernard Leach *A Potter's Book* Faber & Faber

H. Fraser *Kilns and Kiln Firing for the Craft Potter* Pitman

INDEX